10 Unison Songs in 10 Rhythmic Styles with Optional Rhythm Band Parts

Words and Music
by Sally K. Albrecht

Recording Orchestrated
and Produced
by Alan Billingsley

Contents

Alfred

Alfred Music Publishing Co., Inc.
P.O. Box 10003
Van Nuys, CA 91410-0003
alfred.com

ISBN-10: 0-88284-840-2 (Book & CD)
ISBN-13: 978-0-88284-840-2 (Book & CD)

ISBN-10: 0-7390-8351-1 (Book)
ISBN-13: 978-0-7390-8351-2 (Book)

Illustration: Scott Angle
Art Direction / Design: Holly DeBord

NOTE: The purchase of this book carries with it the right to reprint pages 40–71 only. Not for resale.

How to Use This Book

Rhythm to the Rescue! is a practical and versatile publication, combining clever songs with a dynamic way to develop rhythmic reading and stylistic concepts.

As a Songbook . . .

The 10 songs in this collection feature 10 different musical styles with lyrics that describe the style. Together, they form an entertaining performance program (approx. 15 minutes). You may wish to "bookend" the show by performing the title song "Rhythm to the Rescue!" as an opening <u>and</u> closing number. Vocal ranges are moderate (middle C up to D an octave above). Reproducible Song Sheets are located on pages 40-47. The songs may be performed with piano accompaniment or SoundTrax CD/Cassette, with or without the Rhythm Band Parts.

Adding Rhythm Instruments . . .

Each song has a variety of Rhythm Band Parts which may be photocopied for student use (see pages 52-71). The director should first work through the Rhythm Practice guides on pages 50-51 before handing out the individual song parts.

As each selection is prepared:

1. Discuss the time signature, tempo and dynamic markings.

2. Look through one rhythm part at a time, reviewing the Rhythm Practice guides as needed.

3. Chant, clap and/or tap one part at a time. Students may make vocal sounds that resemble the rhythm instruments indicated.

4. Play the piano accompaniment with each part separately (or use the SoundTrax Cassette or CD), try chanting first, then with rhythm instruments. If using the SoundTrax, you will hear clicks giving the tempo indication.

5. Split the students into two or more parts and repeat the above process.

6. Combine all instrumental parts with the accompaniment.

7. Add singers (if desired), making sure that the rhythm band doesn't cover up the vocals! Half the class can sing, half can play—then trade!

NOTE: Most of the songs are scored for Bells, Triangle, Tambourine, Sticks, Wood Block, Claves, Castanets, Drums and Cymbals. The director may use other available instruments that fit in with the instrumentation (i.e. finger cymbals should play the bell part.)

Rhythm to the Rescue!

The Songs:
Full Scores

1. RHYTHM TO THE RESCUE!

* Optional text when using Rhythm Band instruments.

9
F   Gm   Fm7 Gm F   N.C.
When you're walk-in' down the street, __
Rhy-thm can be   lots of fun. __
Rhy-thm comes __ to the res-cue!
(Band __)
13
B♭   Cm   B♭m7 Cm7 B♭   N.C.
If   you don't know where you are, __
Whole or half or   quar-ter note, __
Rhy-thm comes __ to the res-cue!
(Band __)

17
F
Gm   Fm7 Gm F
N.C.
Three   or   four   beats   to   the   bar, ___
See   what   the   com - pos - er   wrote. ___
Rhy - thm   comes _   to   the
(Band _)
20
21
Bb
res - cue!   When   you've   got _   the   beat ___________   you

23
C
N.C.
must move your feet. Rhy-thm comes to the
(Band)
26
F
res - cue! Rhy-thm comes to the res - cue!
(Band)
8va

2. GIVE ME A BROADWAY TWO-BEAT

* "Give My Regards to Broadway" by George M. Cohan is quoted twice in this selection.

It makes the au-di-ence smile! Give me a Broad-way two-beat, a
one, two, two-beat. I love that vaude-ville style!

mf
mf
mf
mf
G
Put a hat on my head, ___ and a cane in my hand; ___
mf
C
C#dim7
G
cresc.
G7
Broad - way two-beat is in de - mand! _ Give my re - gards to
cresc.

35
E7
f
A7
D7
A7
Broad - way with a Broad - way two- beat, a one, two,
40
D7
A7
D7
G
two - beat. You can't beat Broad - way style!

3. A JAZZY KIND OF SWING

9
F
G7
C7
F
I just love a jazz-y kind of swing, 'cause I love jazz.
13
mf
mf
mf
Bb6
F6
C7
F
F7
mf
mf
Doot doot doot doot dweet doo dow,
Doot doot doot doot dweet doo dow,

14

17

Bb6   F6   G7   C7

Doot doot doot doot dweet doo dow. Yes, I love jazz!

21
mp
mp
mp

F   G7   C7   F
mp

I just love _ a jazz-y kind of swing, a jazz-y kind of swing is real-ly quite the thing.

mp

25
F   G7   C7   Am7♭5   D7
I just love _ a jazz-y kind of swing, 'cause I love jazz! Yes
cresc.
29
f
G   C   F6
I   love   jazz!

4. WHEN WE LEARN TO MARCH
(A 3-Part Round)

* New group begins as 1st group reaches "*"

7
(On repeat, vamp last two measures until all voices are done.)
(On repeat, vamp last two measures until all voices are done.)
*
March, two, three, four, march! Let's go! March, two, three, four, march! Let's go!
(On repeat, vamp last two measures until all voices are done.)

5. A SEA CHANTY

might be-come a sail-or ____ and learn a song or two.
pitch - es are quite sim-ple; ____ you sing it with great flair.
A
sea chant - y, sea chant - y, here's what you must do: is be -

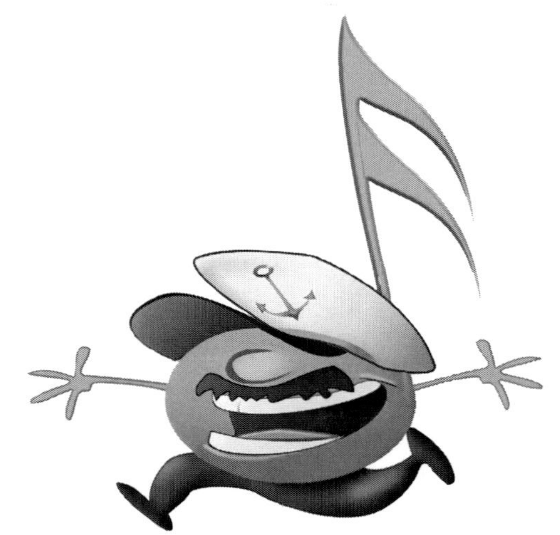

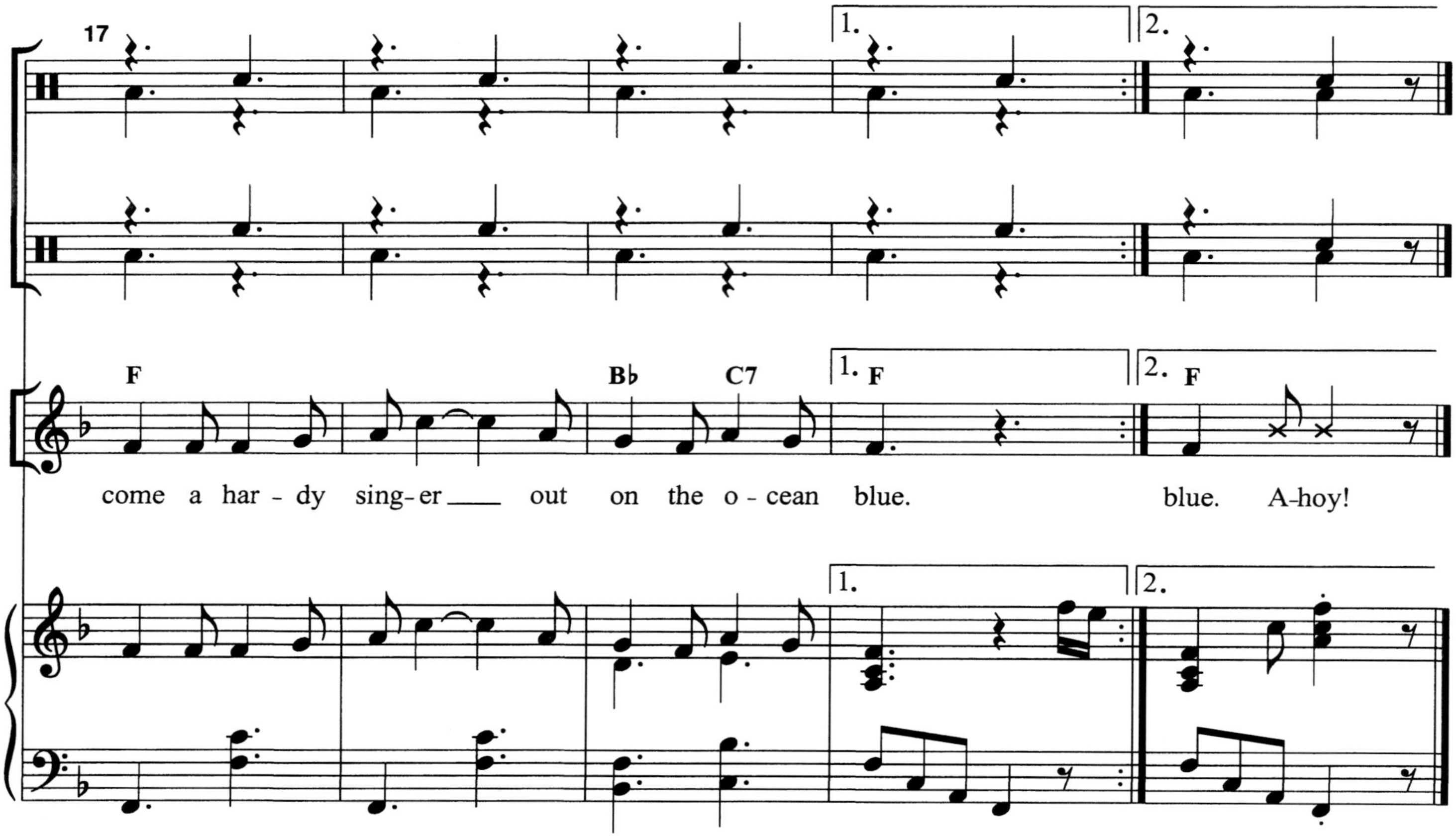
17
1.
2.
F
Bb
C7
1. F
2. F
come a har - dy sing - er ___ out on the o - cean blue.
blue. A-hoy!

6. I GOT THE BLUES

9
Bb
F
spend some time with you, ___ then I would know just what to do. ___
join me in this song, ___ then I would know that I be - long. ___
13
C7
Bb7
F6
C7
Got the blues down to my shoes. I got the blues.
Oh well, I
2. I got the

decresc. e rit.
17
p
decresc. e rit.
p
p
decresc. e rit.
F6
C7
F7
p (whisper)
blues.
I got the blues.
Yeah!
decresc. e rit.
p

7. WE WANT TO HEAR A WALTZ

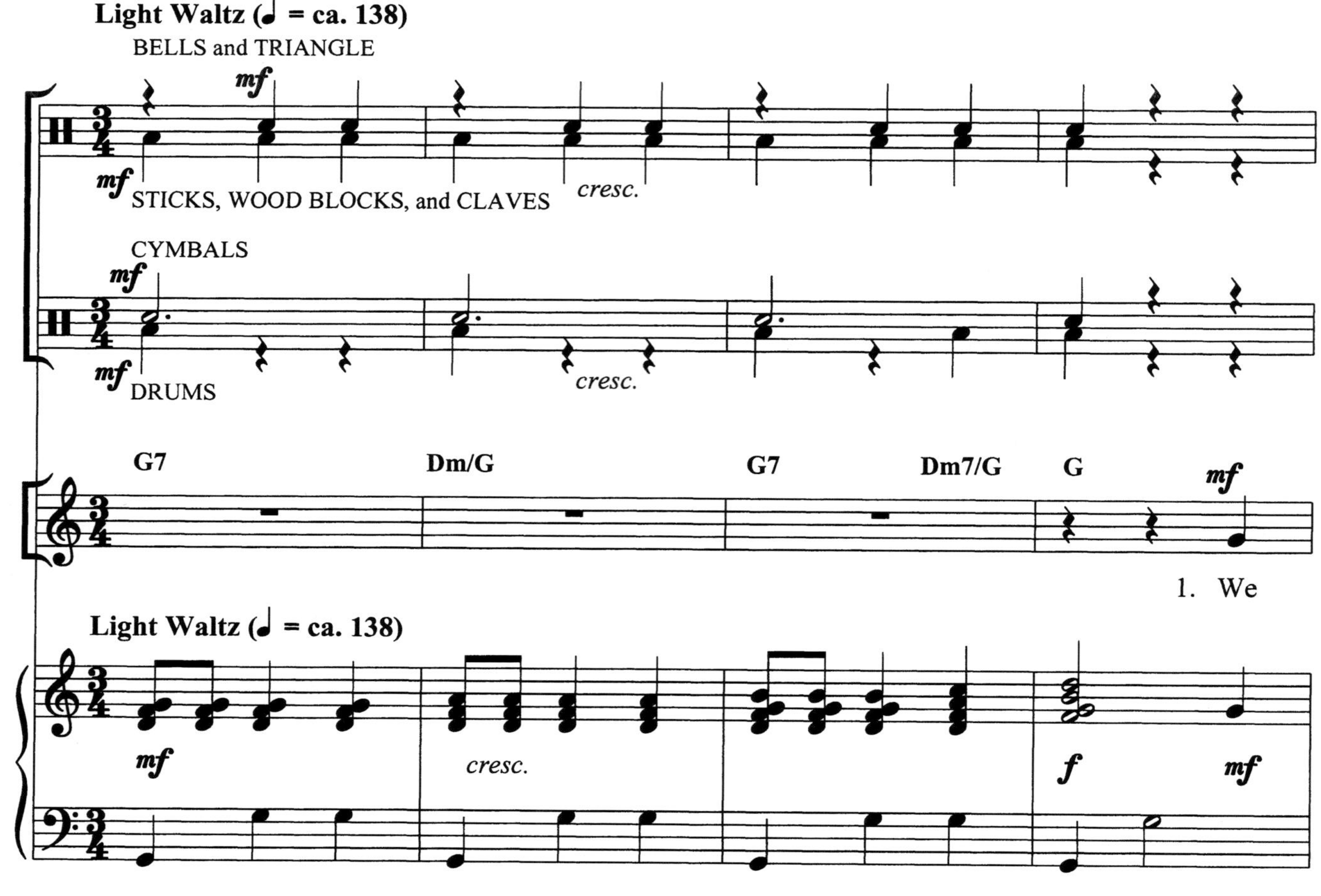

9
1. after D.S., to CODA
G7
1. C after D.S., to CODA
D9
G7
1. after D.S., to CODA
one, two, three, dance with me, love - ly, flow - ing waltz. The
13 2.
14
2. C
F
2.
waltz. We'll sway from left to right,

17
F
C
and may - be dance all
20
rit.
D.S. al CODA
G
Dm/G
G7
Dm7/G
G7
D.S. al CODA
rit.
mf
night.
We
cresc.
rit.
mf
D.S. al CODA

CODA
24 cresc.
CODA
G7 cresc.
G6
G7
one, two, three, dance with me love - ly, flow - ing
CODA
cresc.
28 f
f
f
f
f
f C
Am
F
G7
C
waltz.

8. CALYPSO!

* Director may wish to continue maracas (eighth note rhythm) through m. 11.

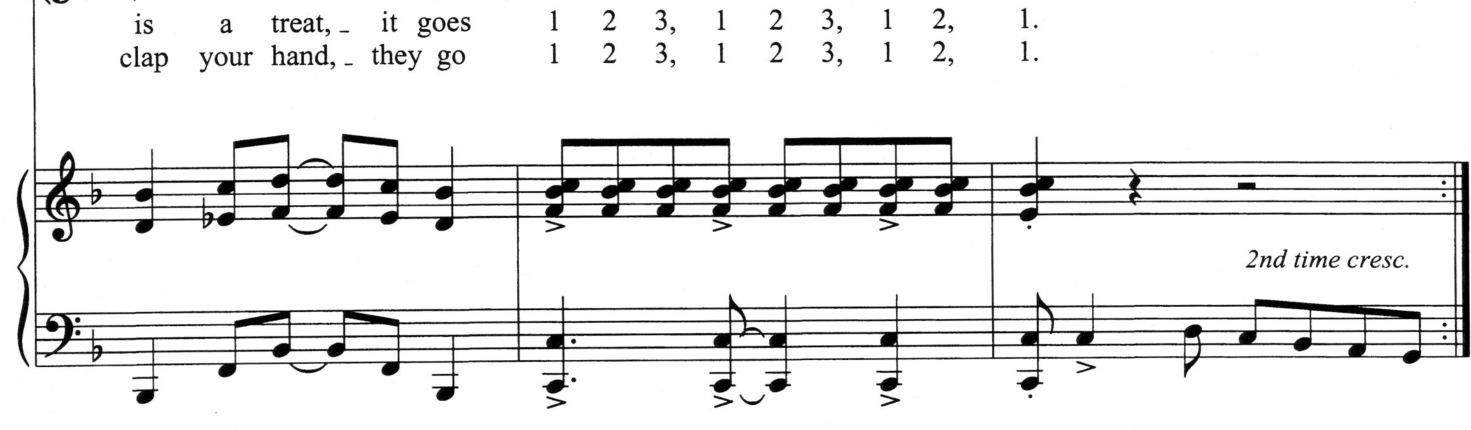
7
C7
F
you be-gin to move your feet. __
where the o-cean meets the land. __
Oh, Ca - lyp - so
Make you want to
10 
mf
Bb
C7sus.
C7
is a treat, _ it goes 1 2 3, 1 2 3, 1 2, 1.
clap your hand, _ they go 1 2 3, 1 2 3, 1 2, 1.
2nd time cresc.

Ca - lyp - so!
Ca - lyp - so!
Ca - lyp - so!
Ay yi yi!

9. SLOW ROCK AND ROLL

Oh, don't you dig it way down in your soul?
Swing - in' and sway - in' to mu - sic we a - dore.
D   Bm7   G6   A7
Just grab a part - ner and you will know
Peo - ple are danc - in' and want - ing more!
D   Bm7   G6   D/F#   Em7b5

9
D/A
A
D/F#
G
Why   we   love   slow rock and   roll.
Oh,   we   love   slow rock and   roll.
11
2nd time, rit.
2nd time, fine
2nd time, rit.
2nd time, fine
D/A
A
Dsus.
D
Why   we   love   slow rock and   roll.
Oh,   we   love   slow rock and   roll.
2nd time, rit.
2nd time, fine

10. OUR COUNTRY HOEDOWN

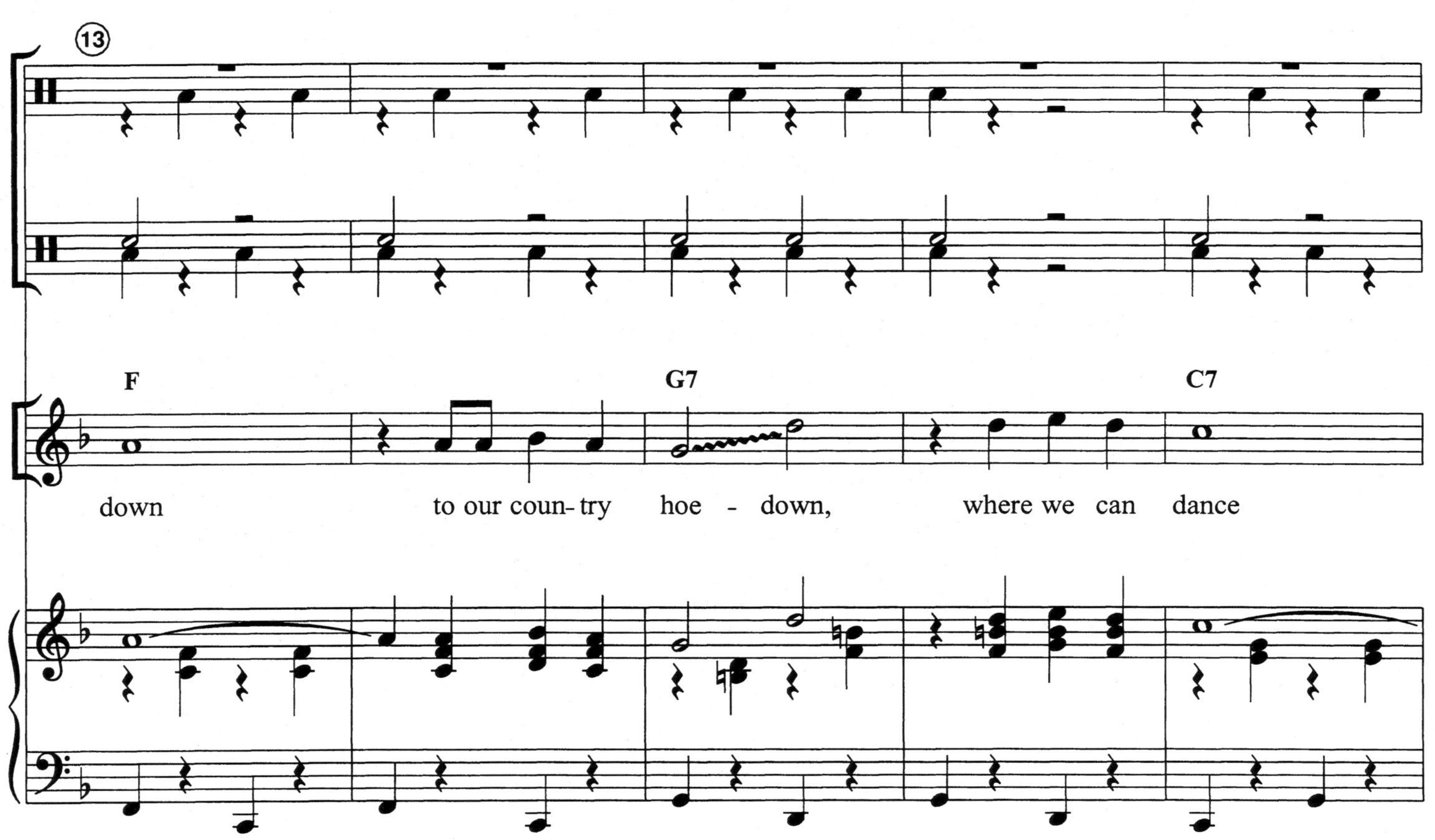

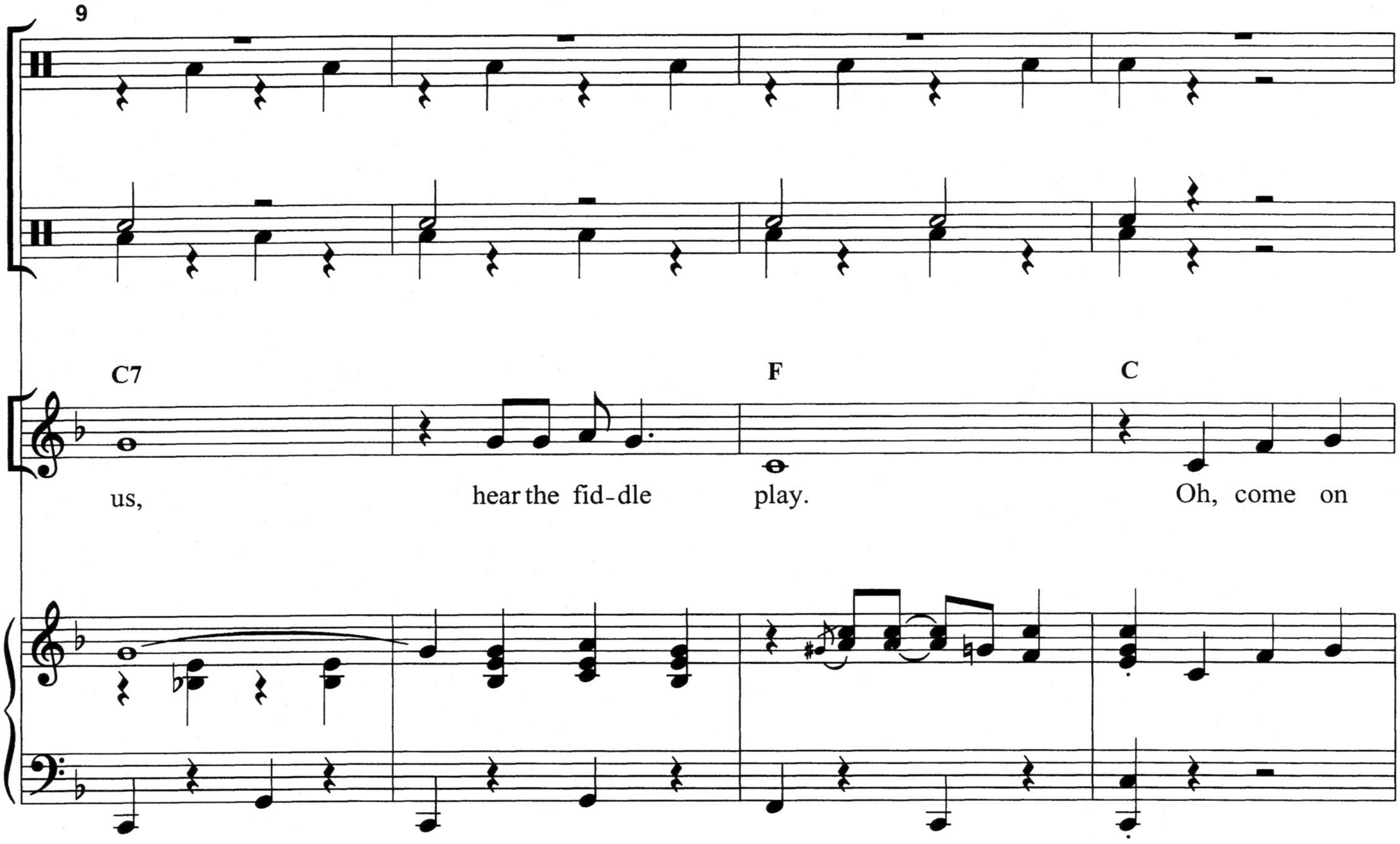
9
C7
F
C
us, hear the fid-dle play. Oh, come on

13
F
G7
C7
down to our coun-try hoe - down, where we can dance

* Banjo-like, detached, nasal singing.

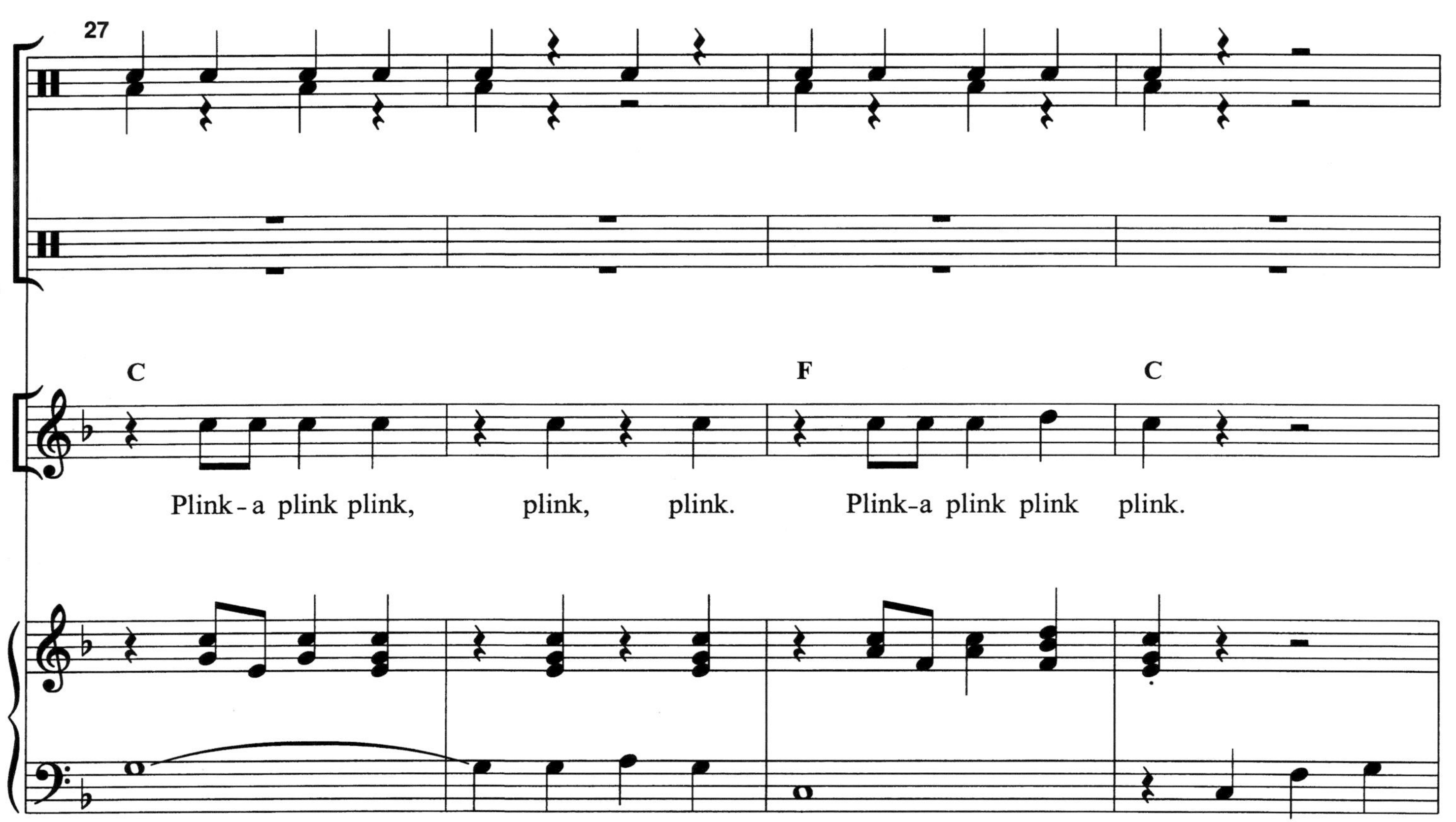

* Banjo "plinks" may continue behind solo caller (repeat meas. 23-30).

* pretty

Rhythm to the Rescue!
Reproducible Song Sheets

1. RHYTHM TO THE RESCUE!

2. GIVE ME A BROADWAY TWO-BEAT

3. A JAZZY KIND OF SWING

4. WHEN WE LEARN TO MARCH

(A 3-Part Round)

March tempo (♩ = ca. 96) *1st time* — sing in unison
2nd time — sing as a 3-part round

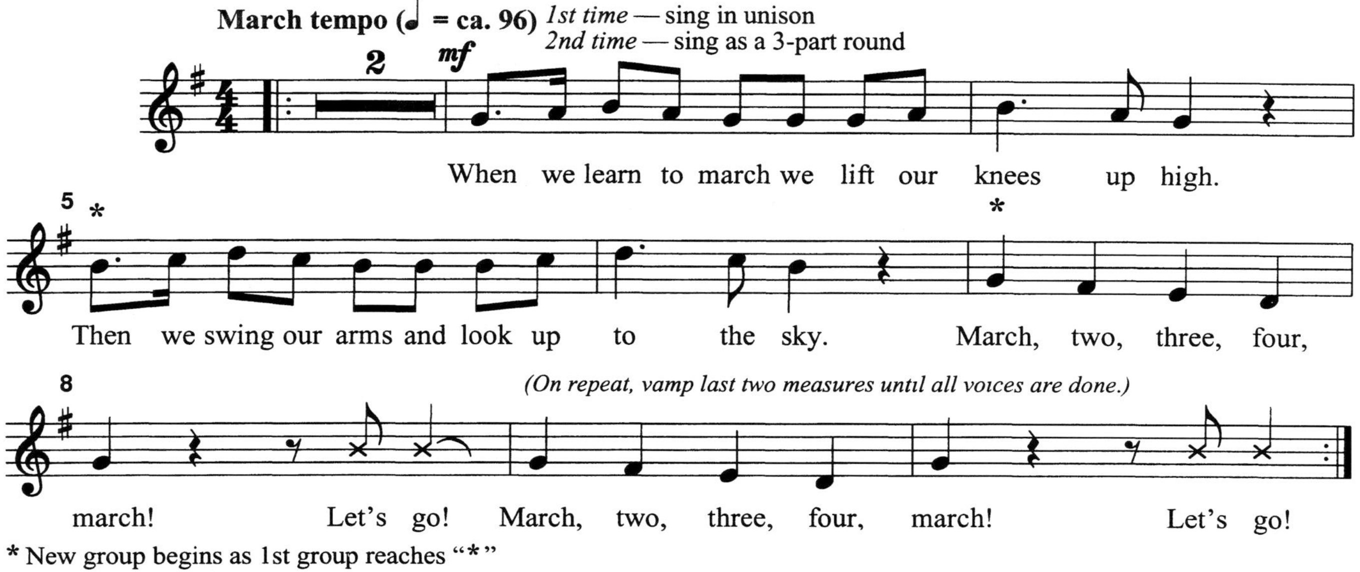

* New group begins as 1st group reaches "*"

5. A SEA CHANTY

With gusto (♩. = ca. 92)

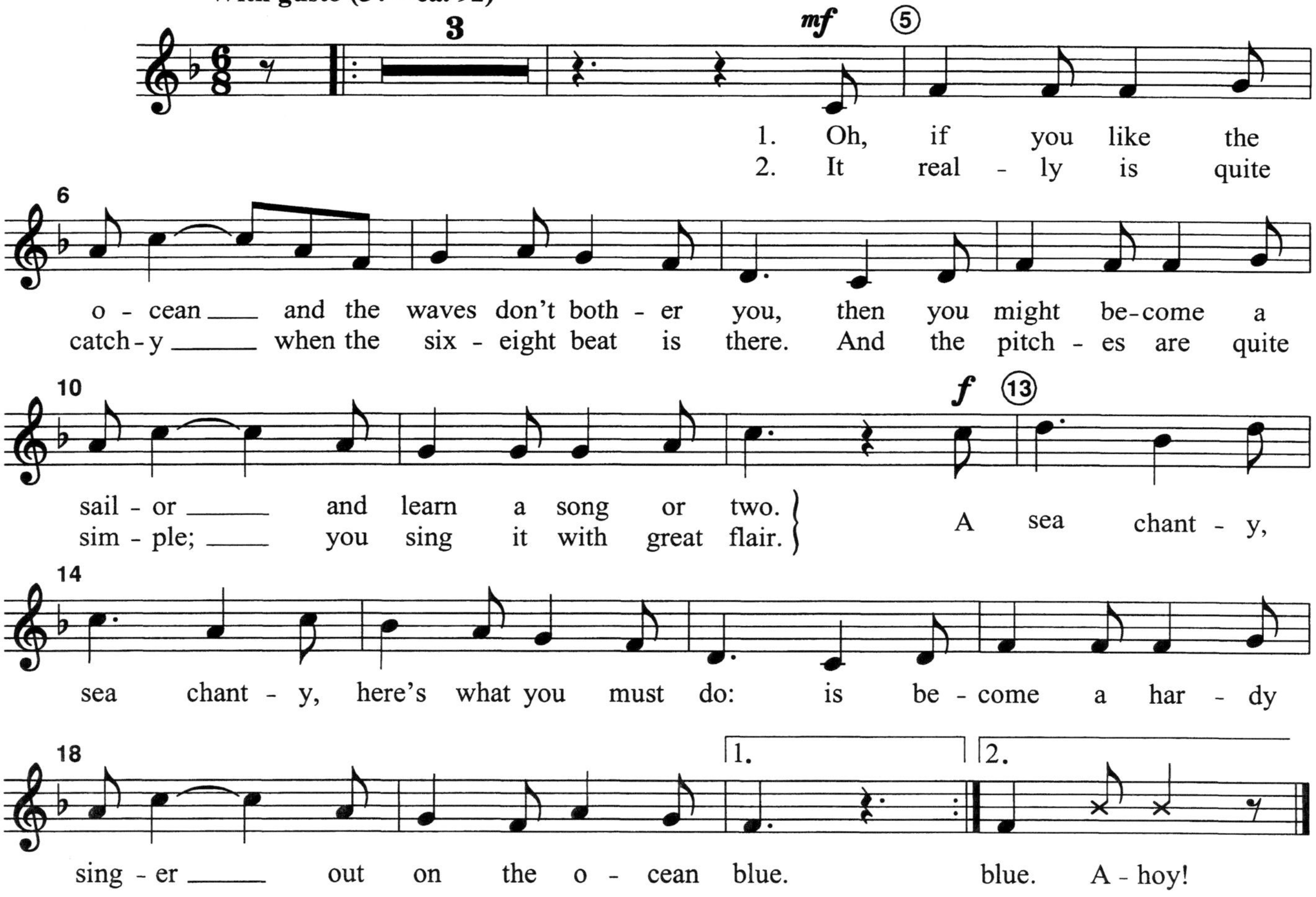

6. I GOT THE BLUES

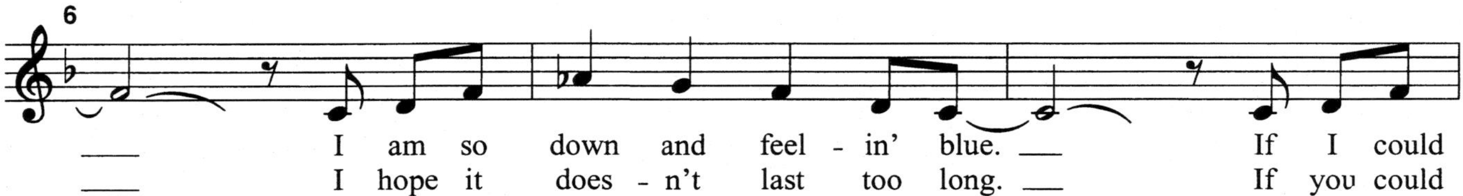

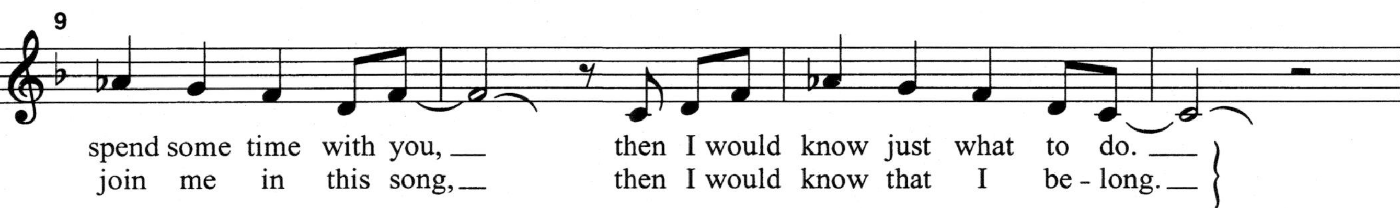

7. WE WANT TO HEAR A WALTZ

8. CALYPSO!

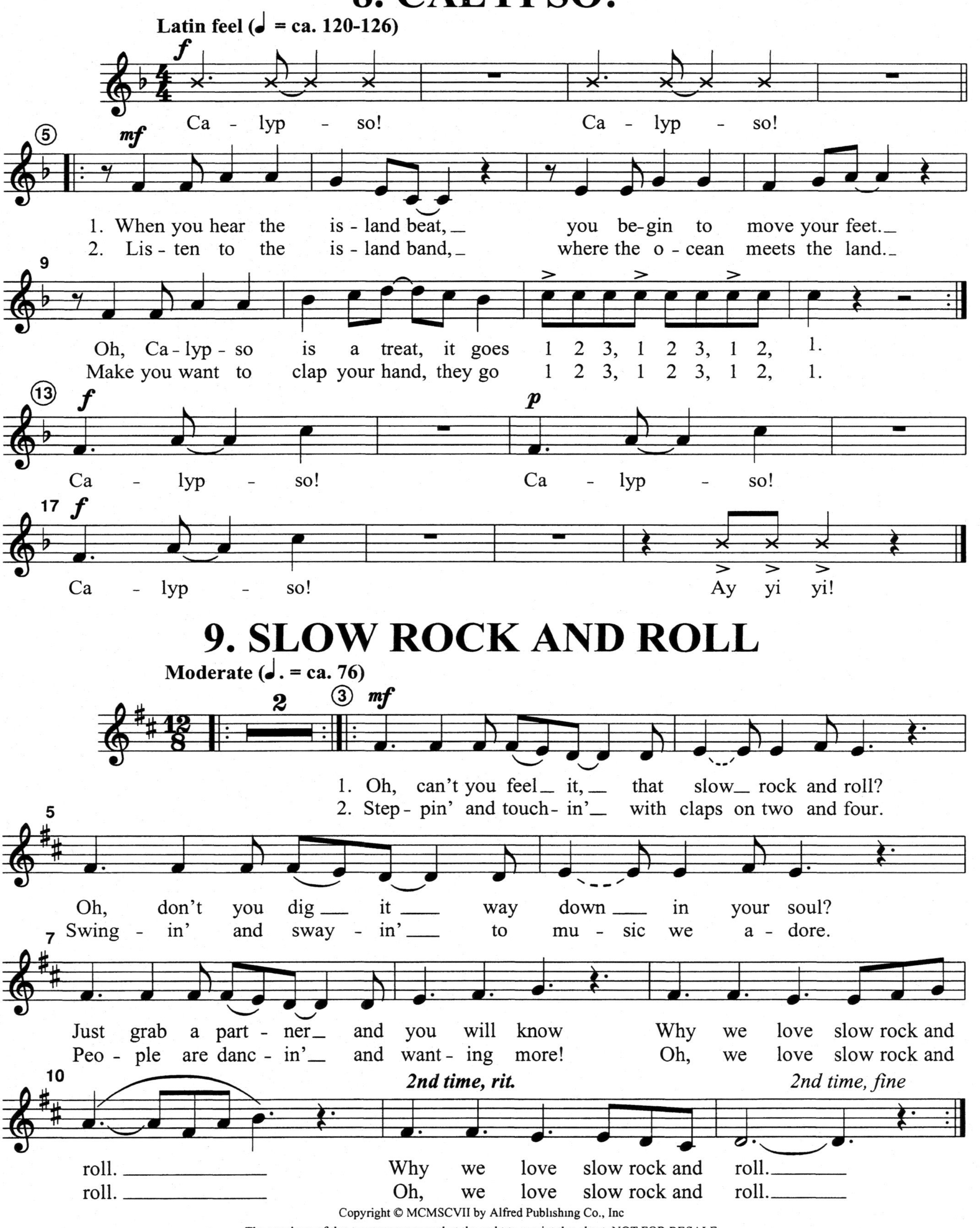

9. SLOW ROCK AND ROLL

10. OUR COUNTRY HOEDOWN

* pretty

Rhythm to the Rescue!

Reproducible
Rhythm Parts

RHYTHM PRACTICE

GROUP A

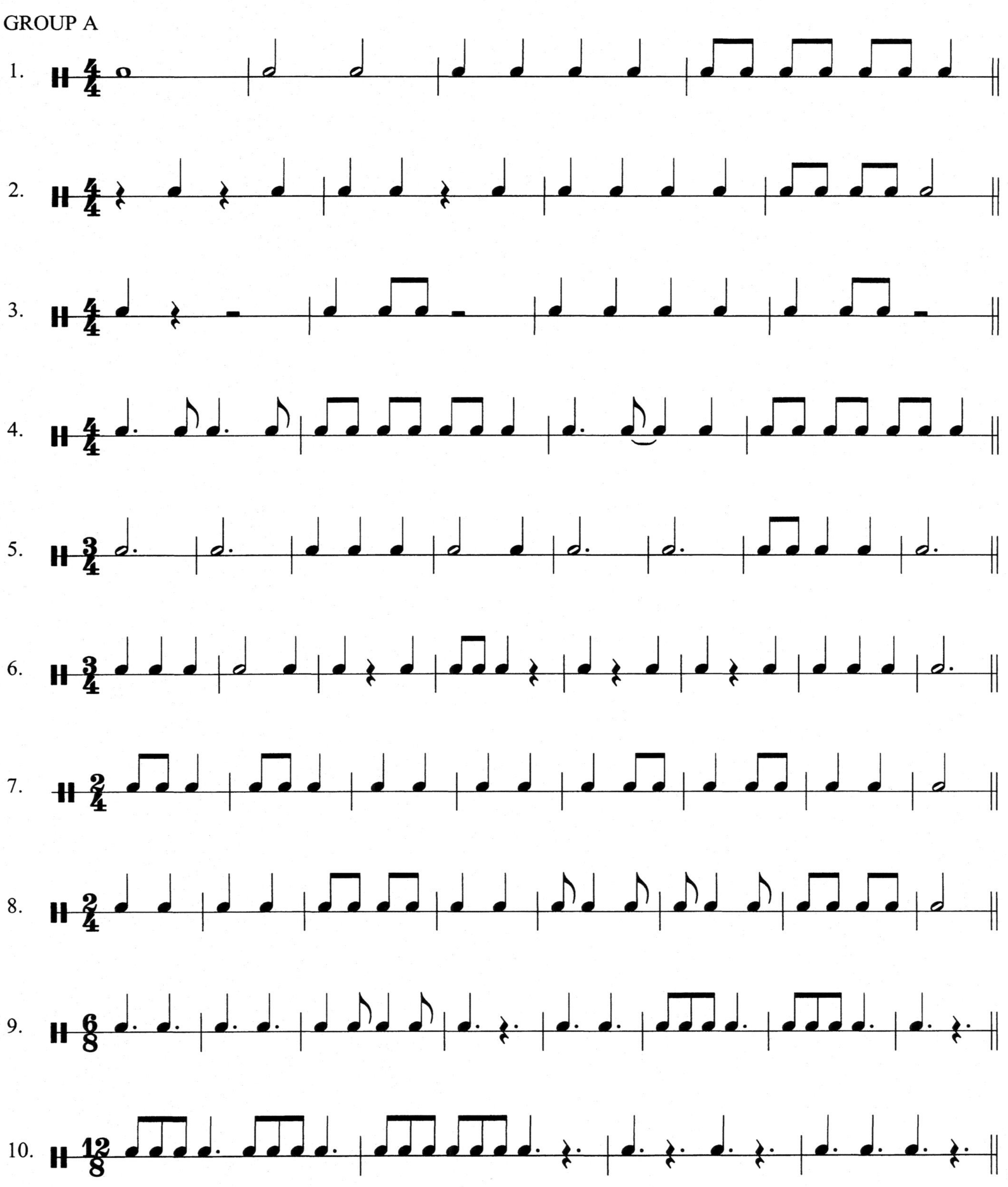

RHYTHM PRACTICE

GROUP B

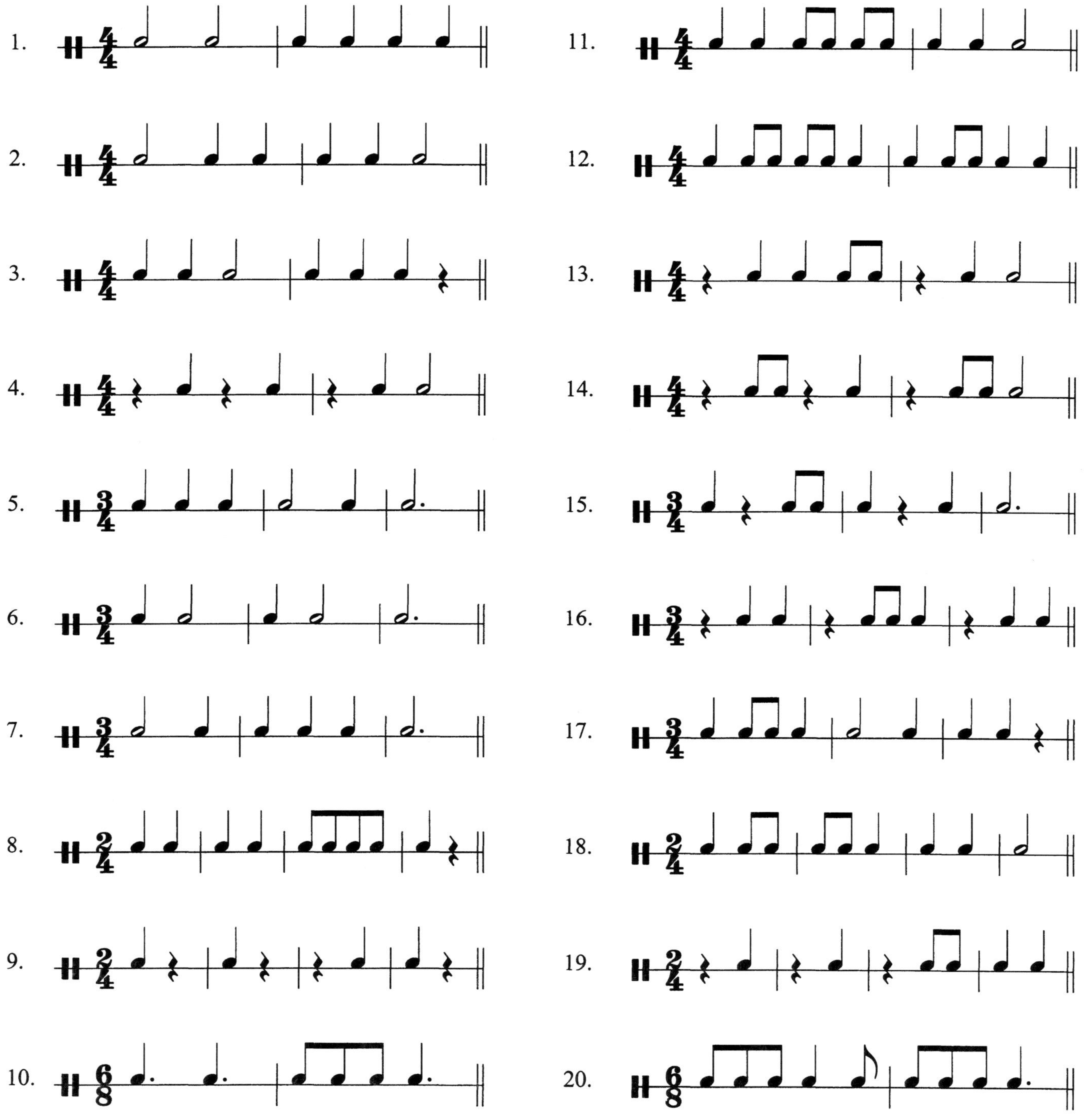

NOTE: For additional exercises, read straight across (i.e., #1 to #11), or mix and match within the same time signature. Try at different tempos.

1. RHYTHM TO THE RESCUE!

BELLS, TRIANGLE and TAMBOURINE

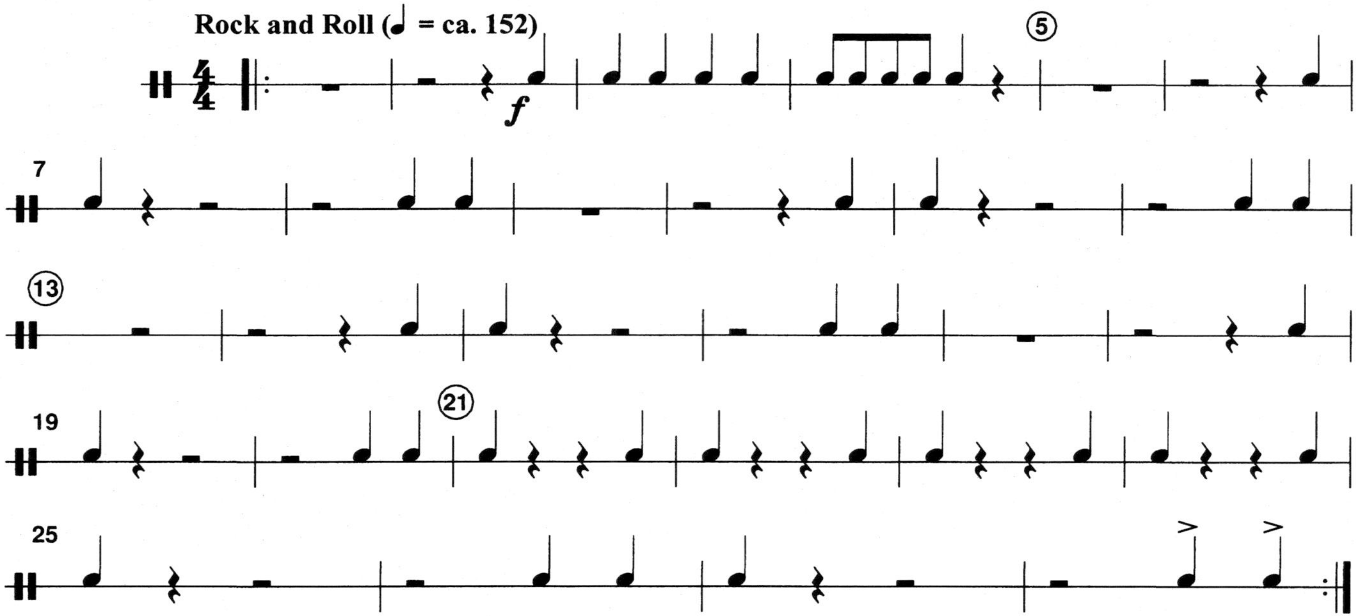

STICKS, WOOD BLOCK and CLAVES

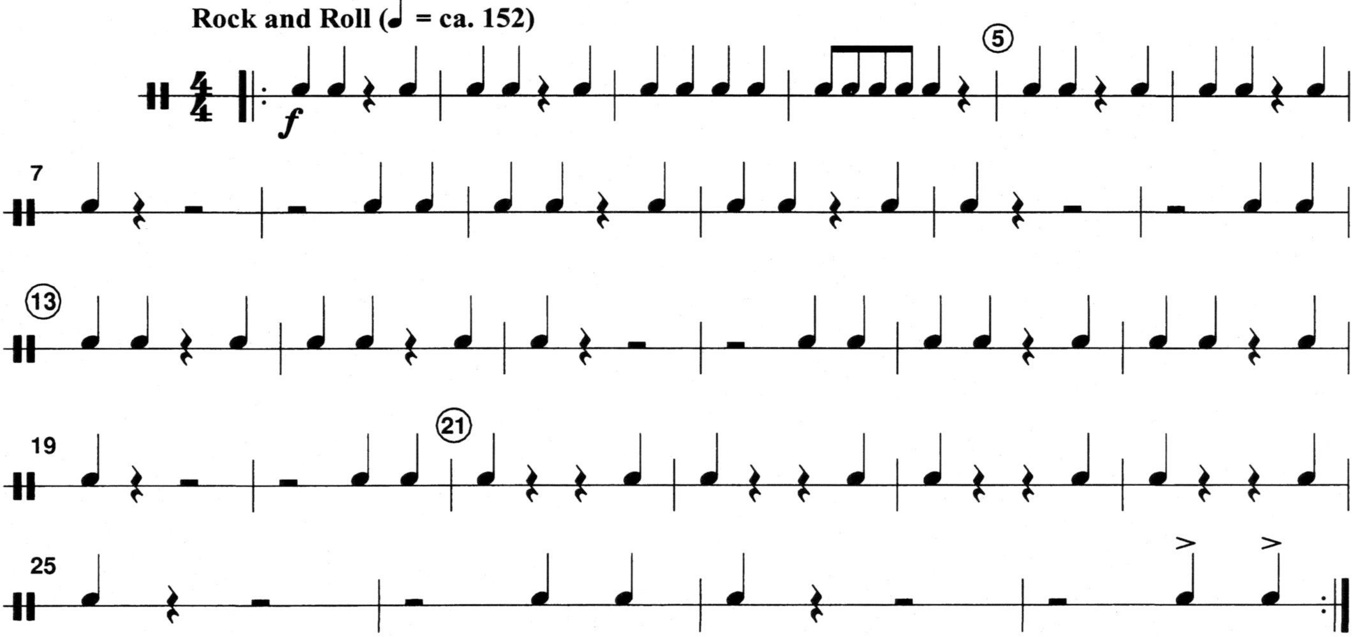

1. RHYTHM TO THE RESCUE!

CYMBALS

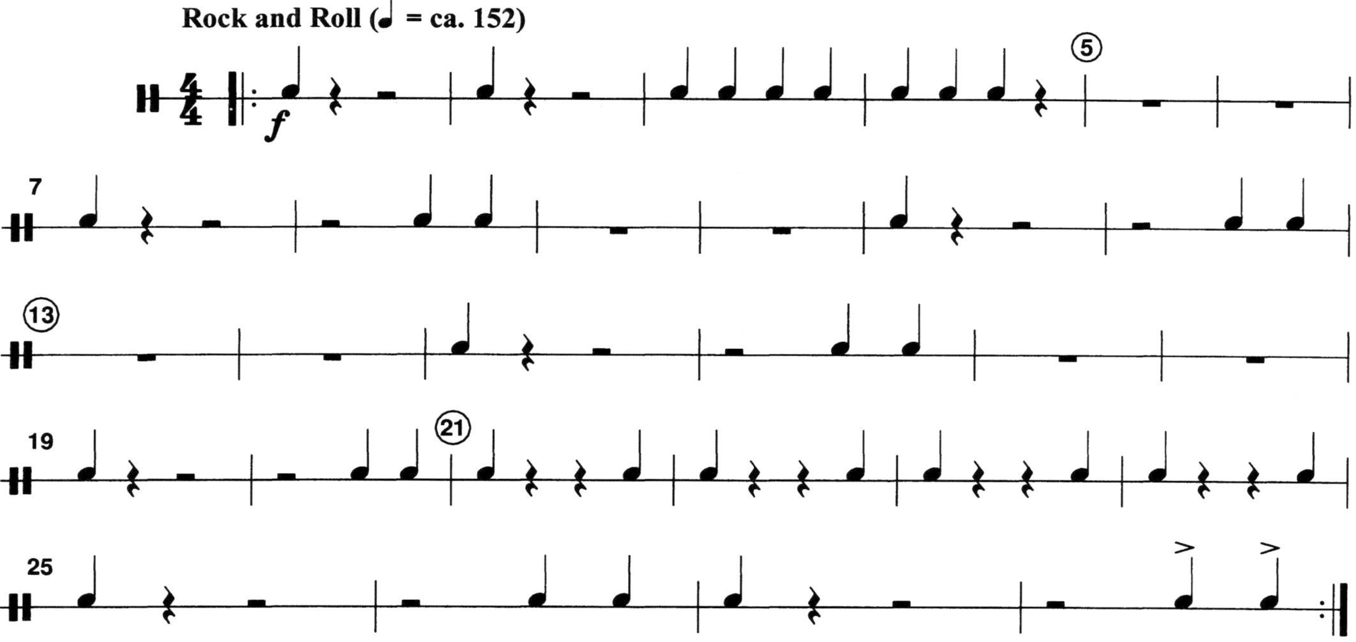

DRUMS

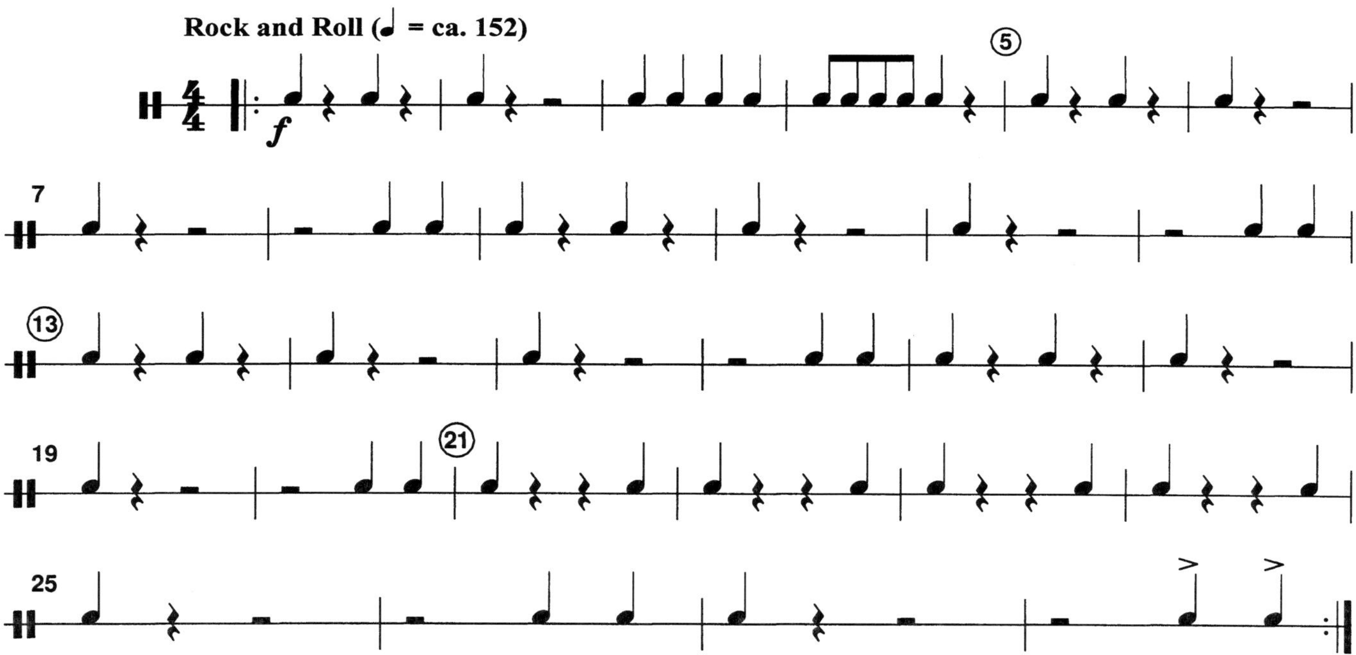

2. GIVE ME A BROADWAY TWO-BEAT

BELLS and TRIANGLE

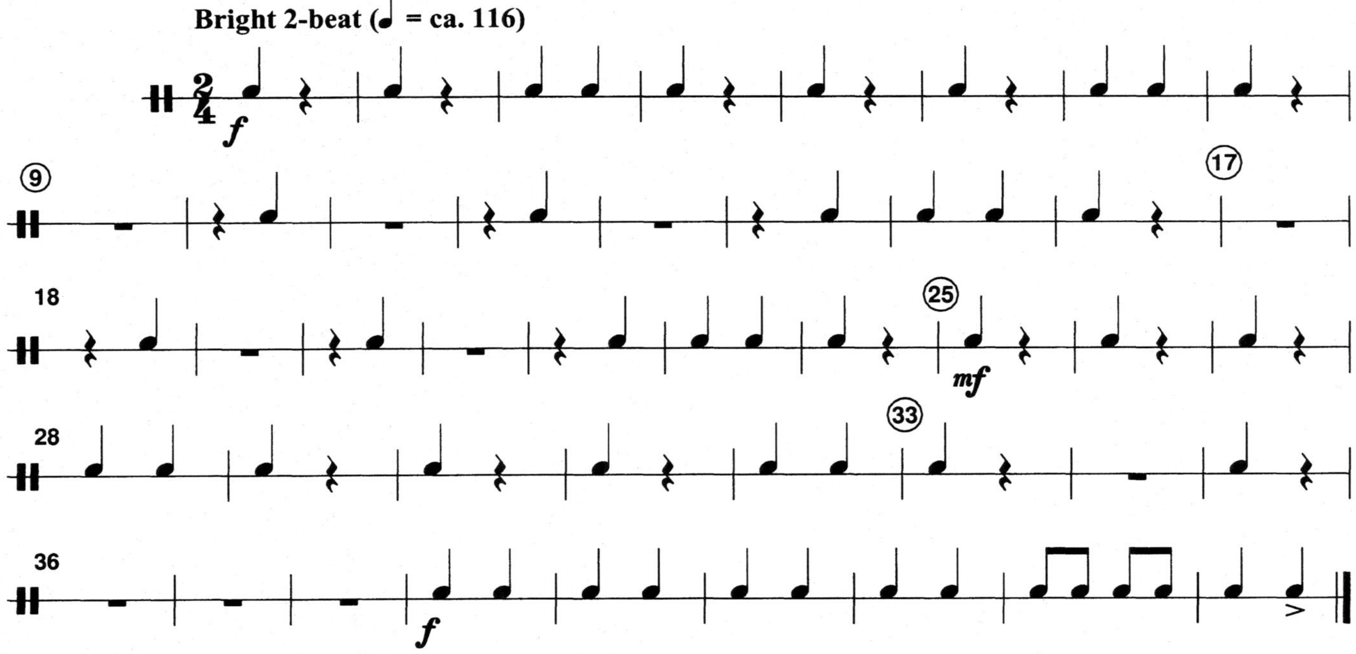

STICKS, WOOD BLOCK and CLAVES

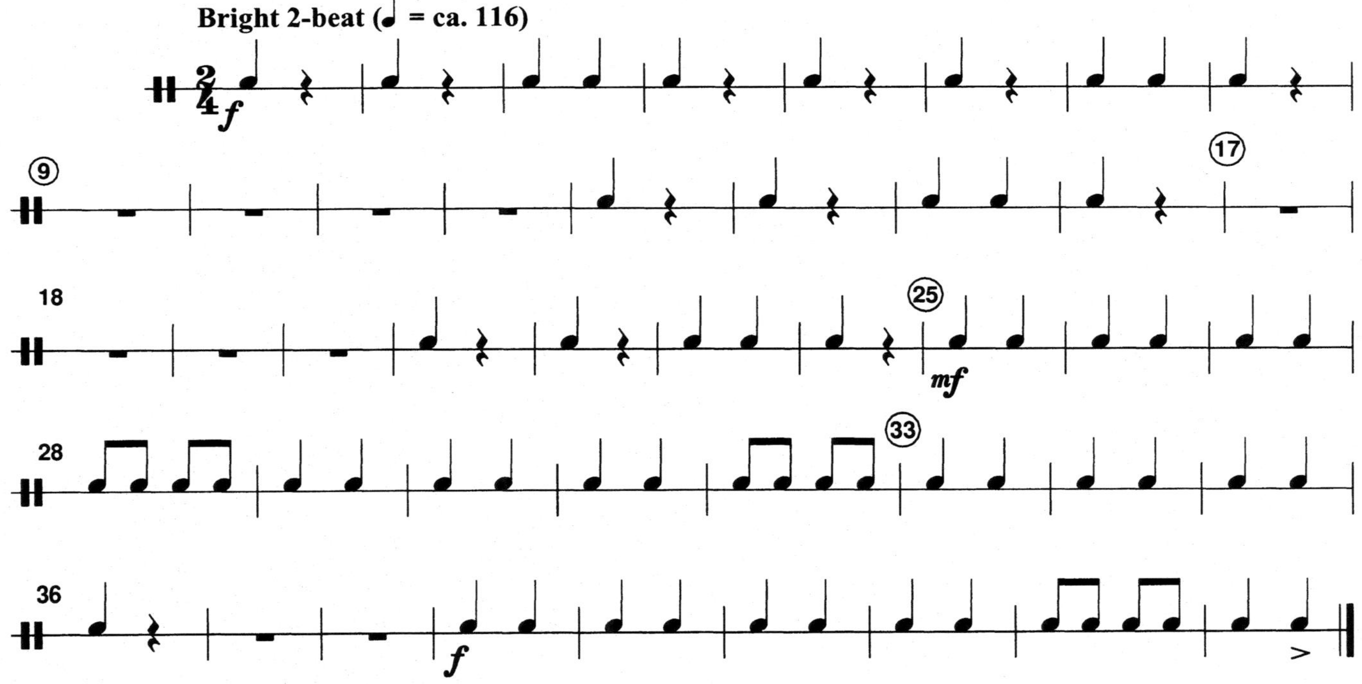

2. GIVE ME A BROADWAY TWO-BEAT

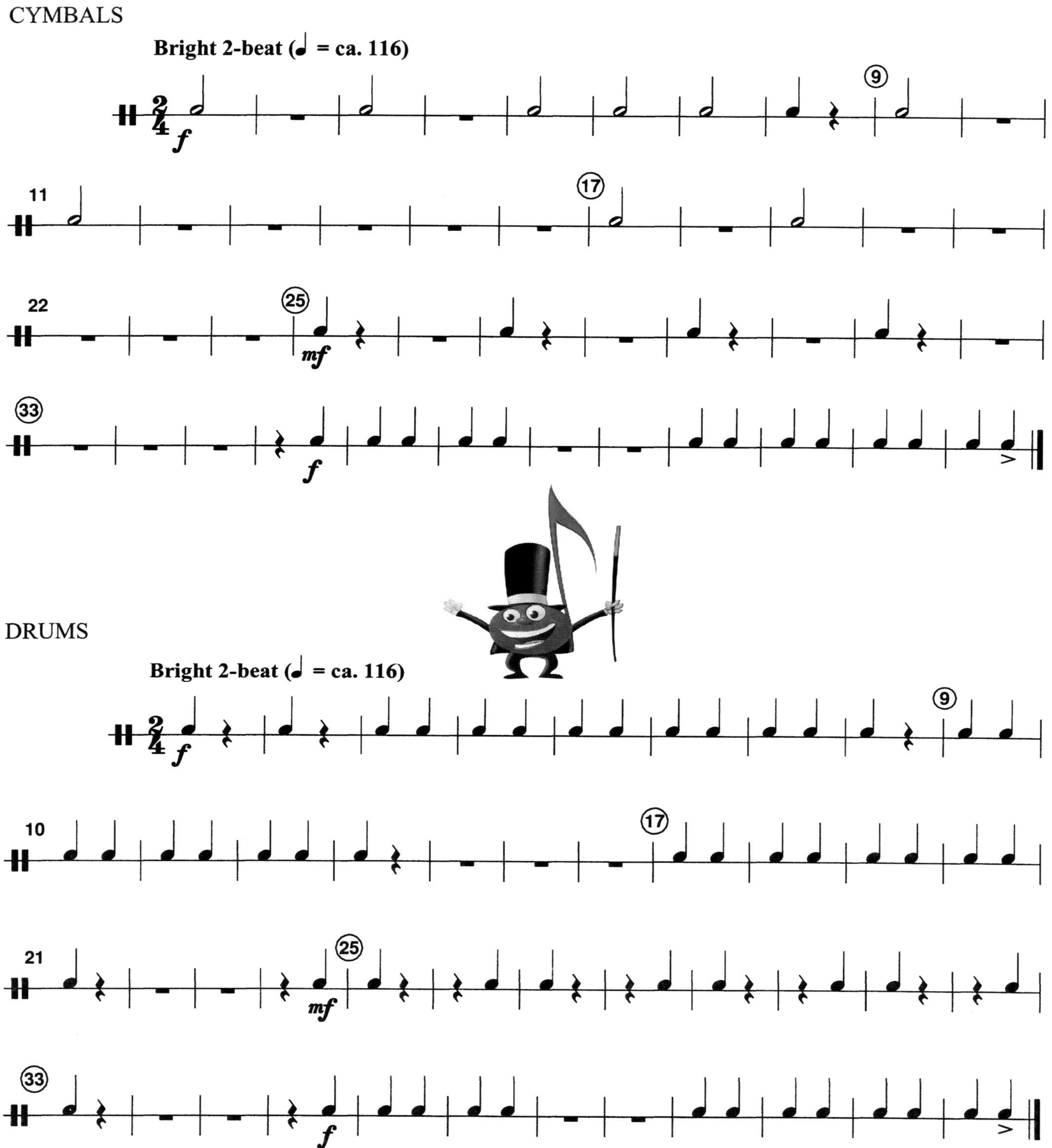

3. A JAZZY KIND OF SWING

BELLS, TRIANGLE and TAMBOURINE

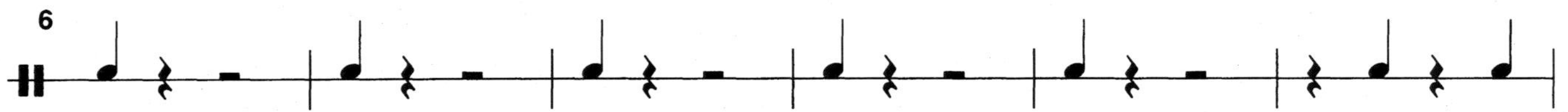

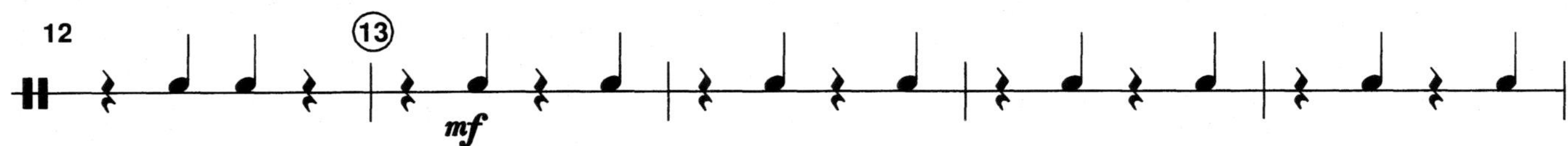

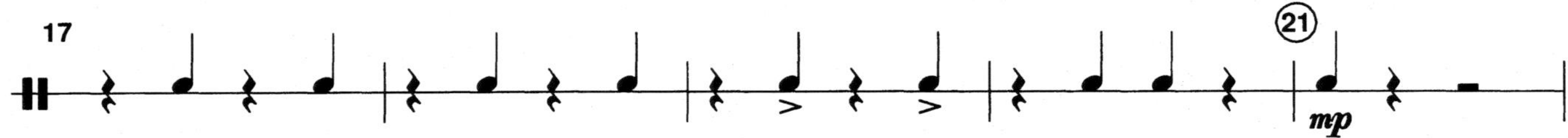

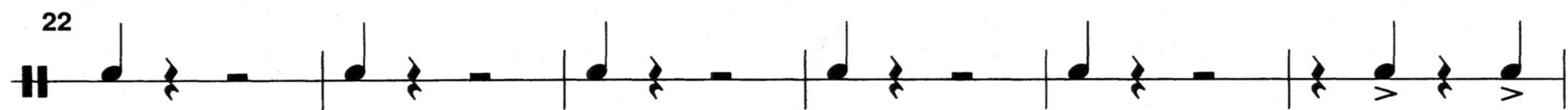

3. A JAZZY KIND OF SWING

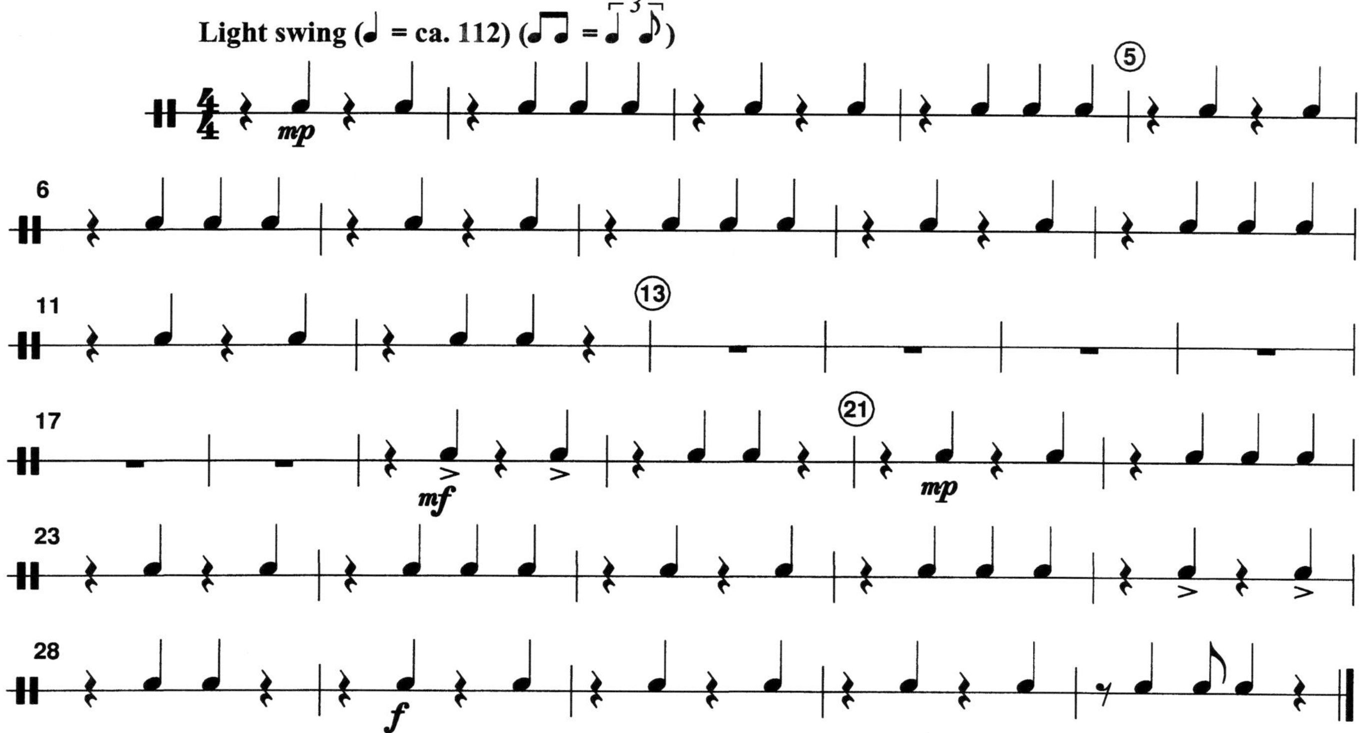

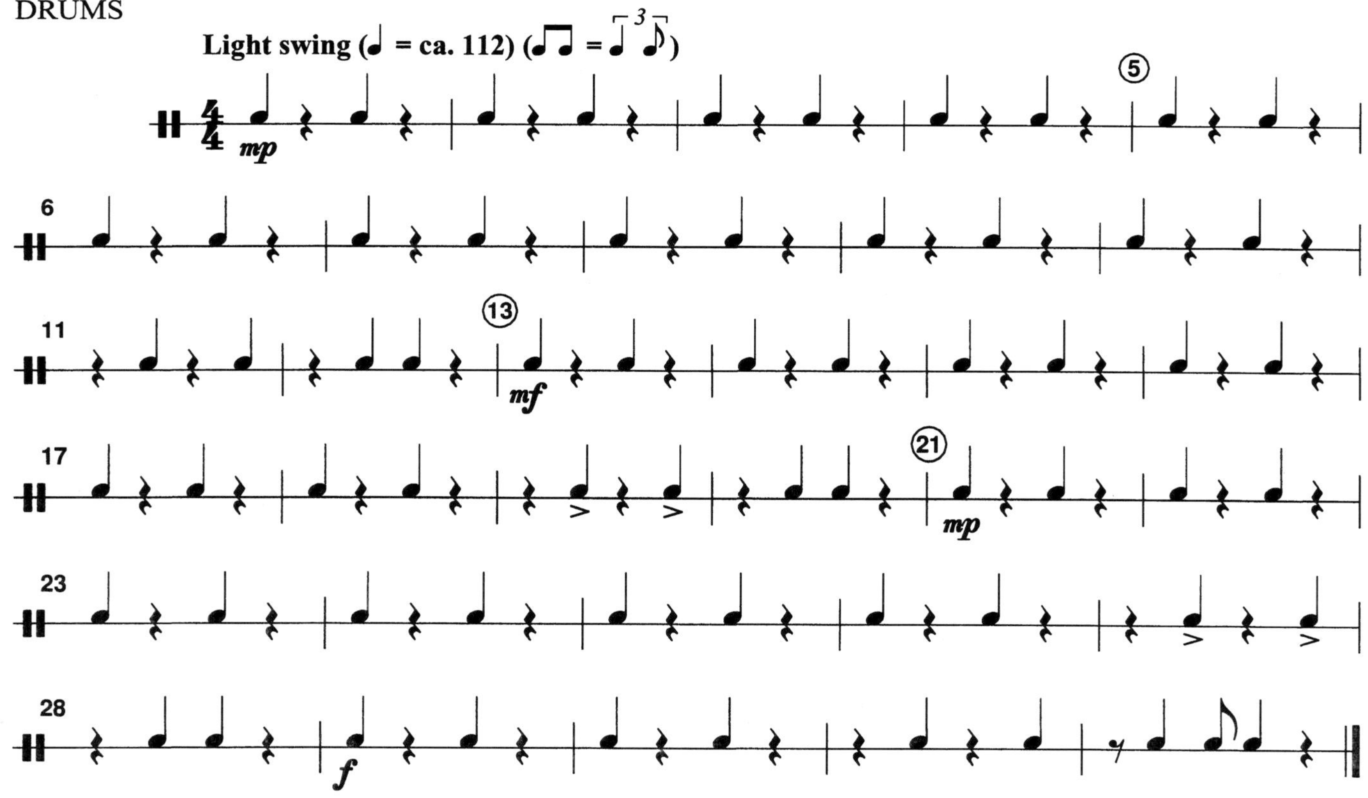

4. WHEN WE LEARN TO MARCH
(A 3-Part Round)

BELLS, TRIANGLE, and TAMBOURINE

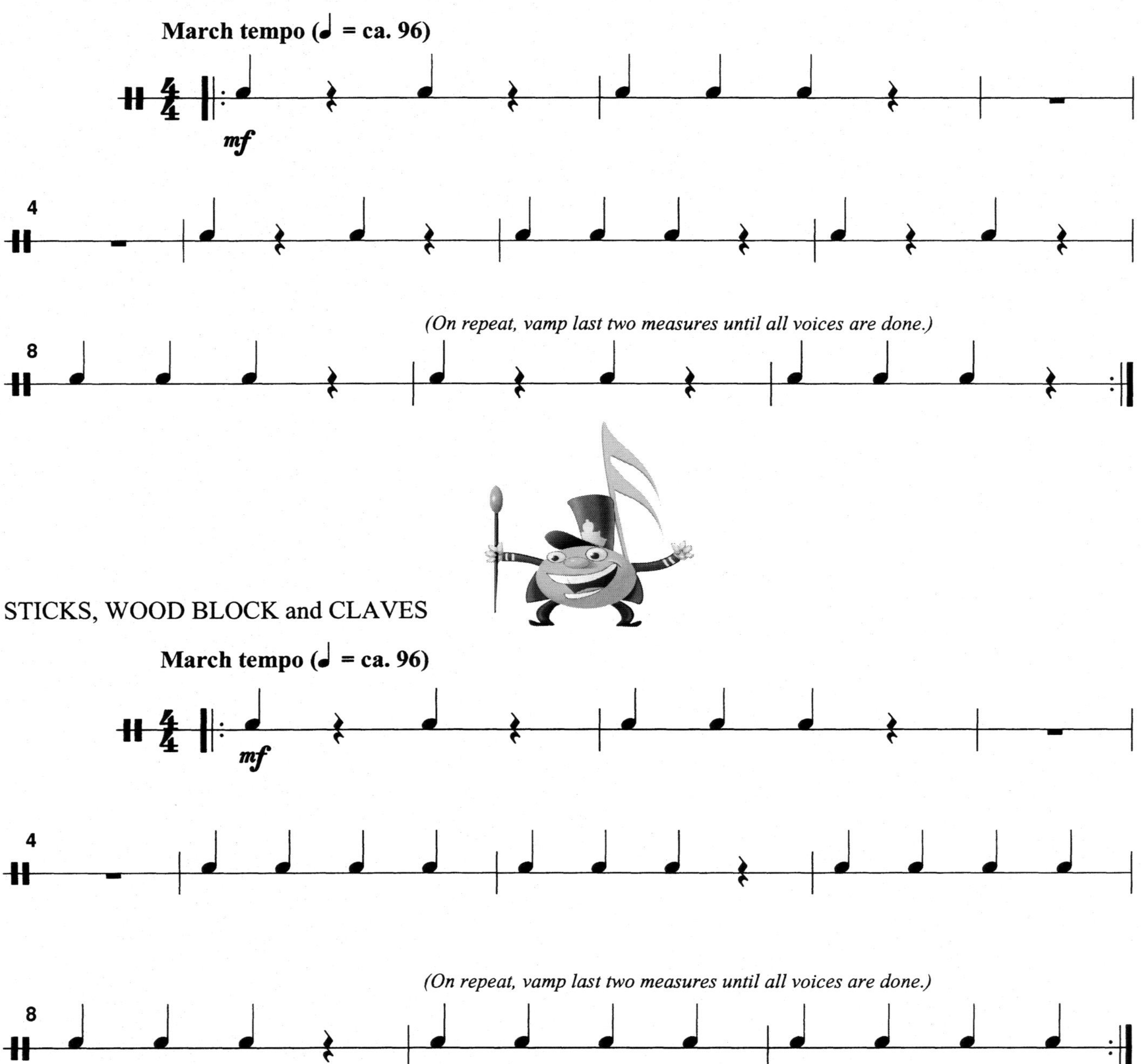

STICKS, WOOD BLOCK and CLAVES

4. WHEN WE LEARN TO MARCH

(A 3-Part Round)

CYMBALS

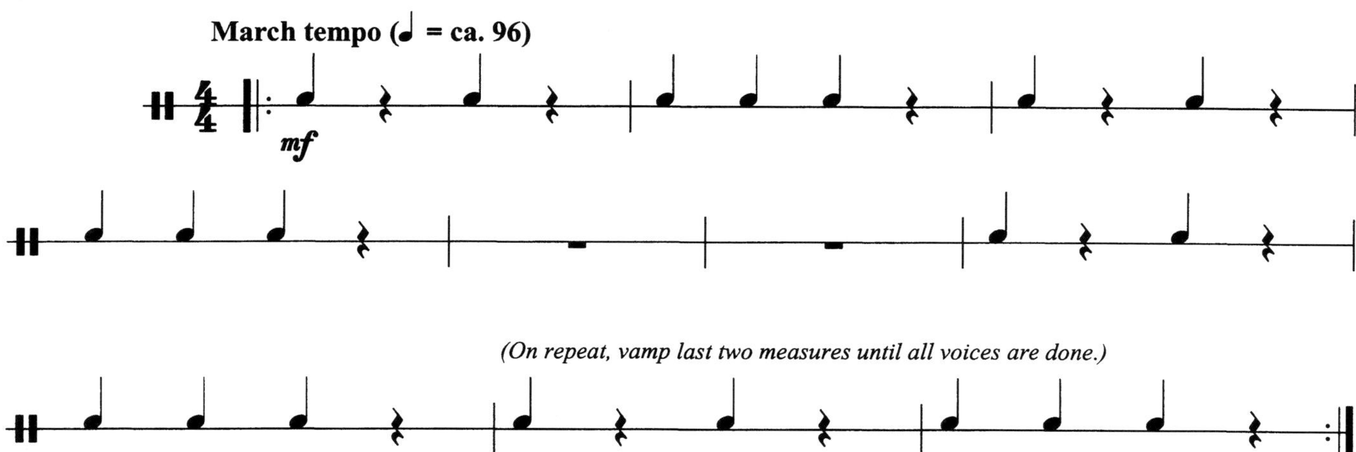

DRUMS

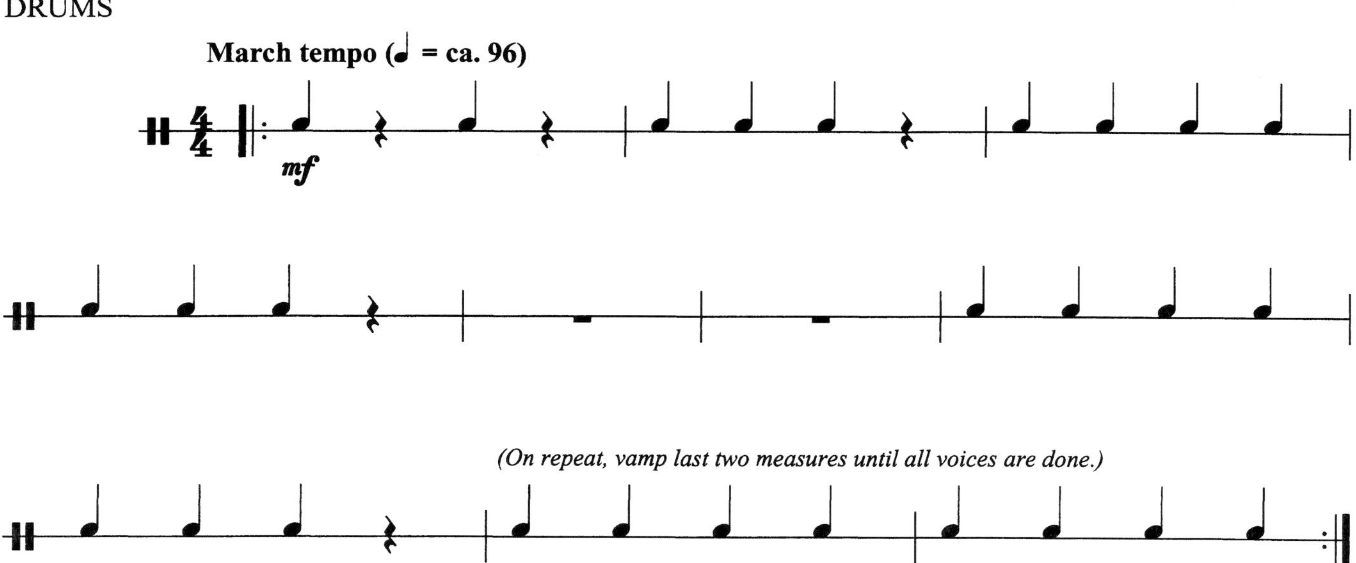

5. A SEA CHANTY

BELLS and TRIANGLE

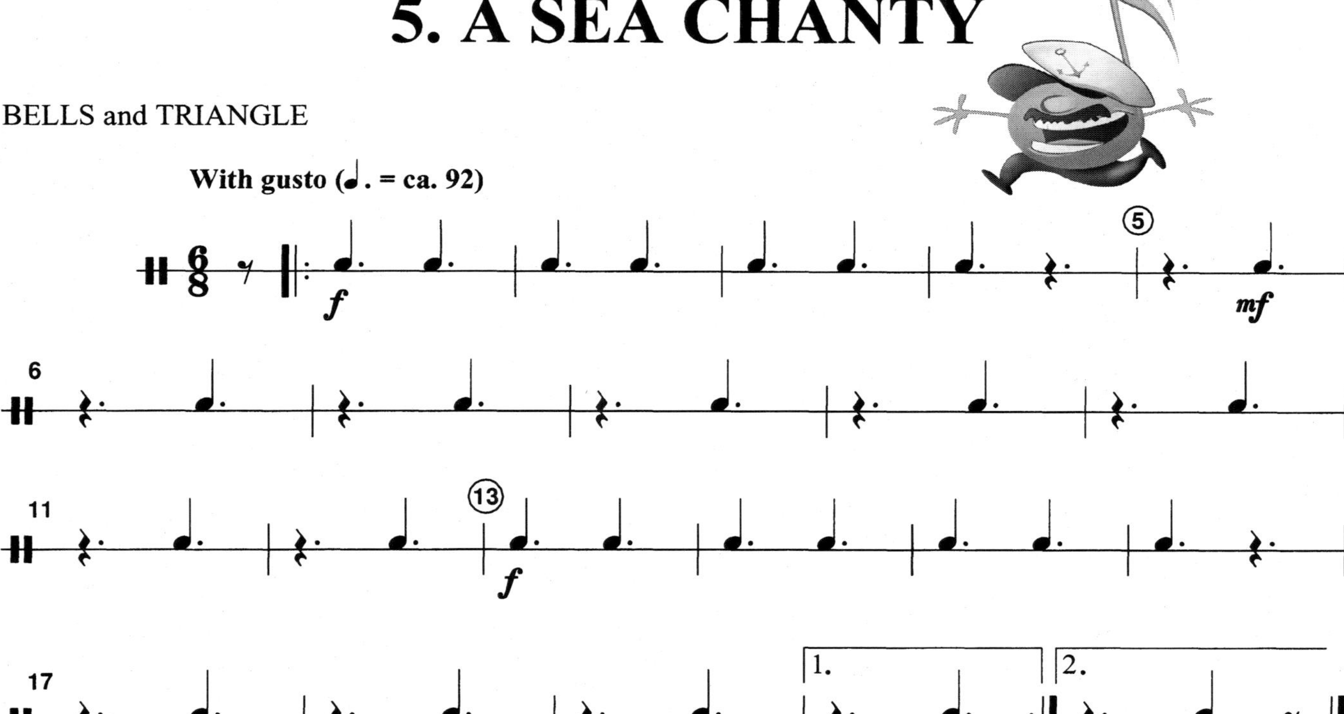

TAMBOURINE

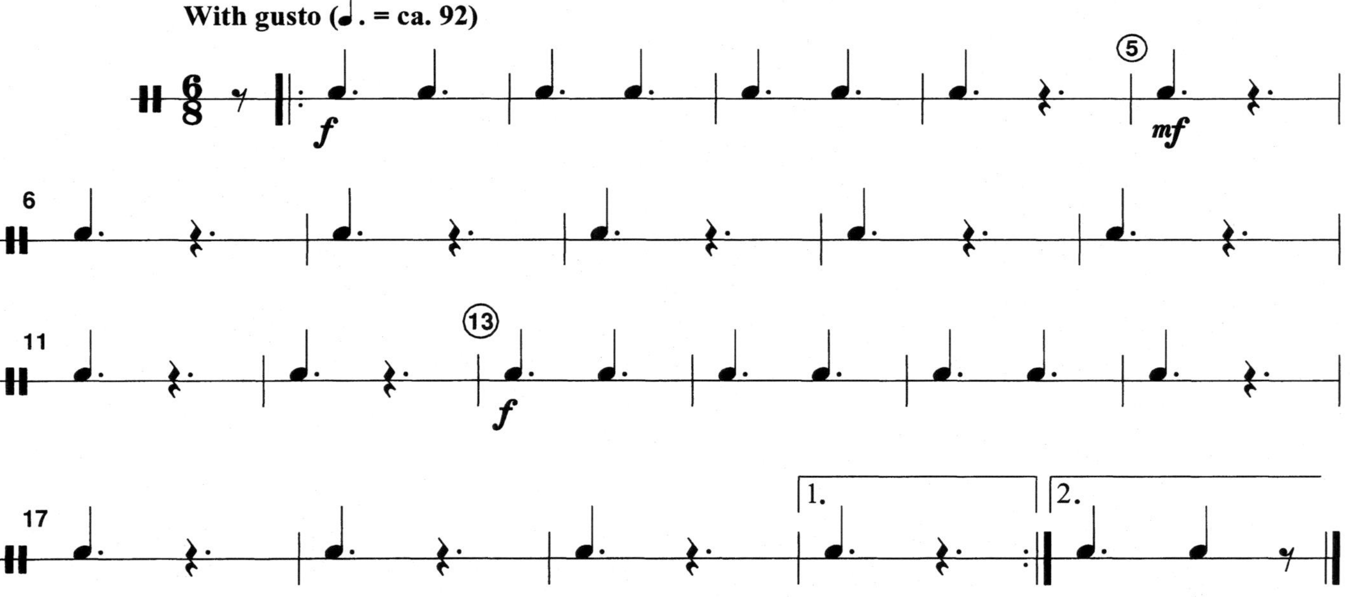

5. A SEA CHANTY

WOOD BLOCK and CLAVES

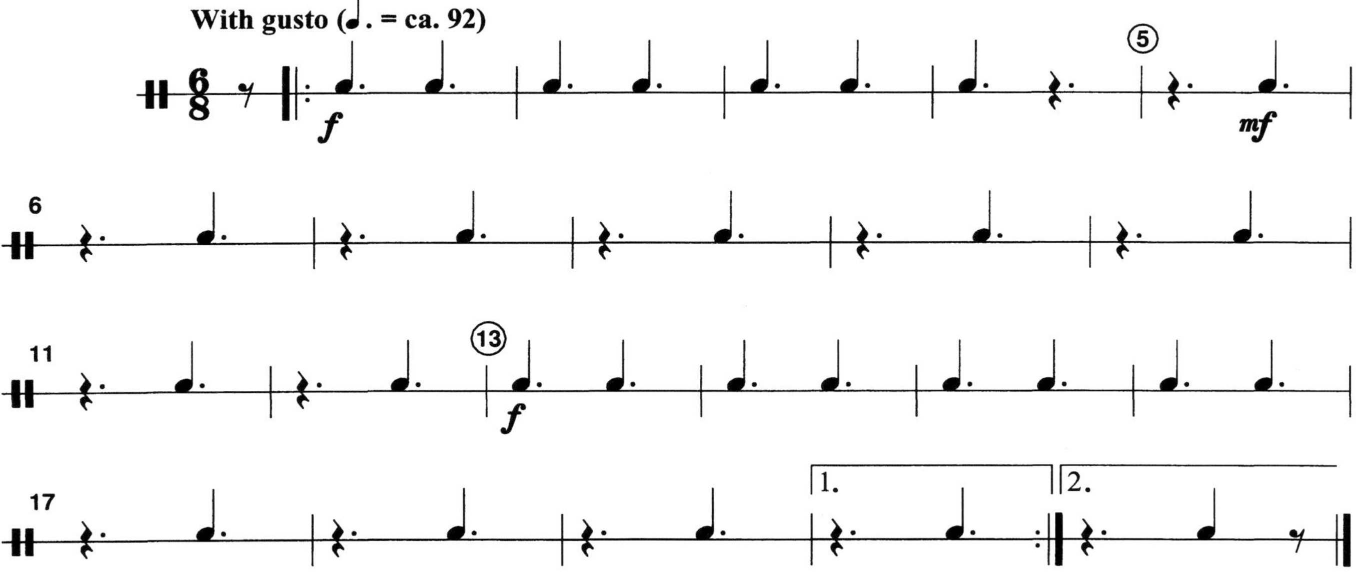

DRUMS and CYMBALS

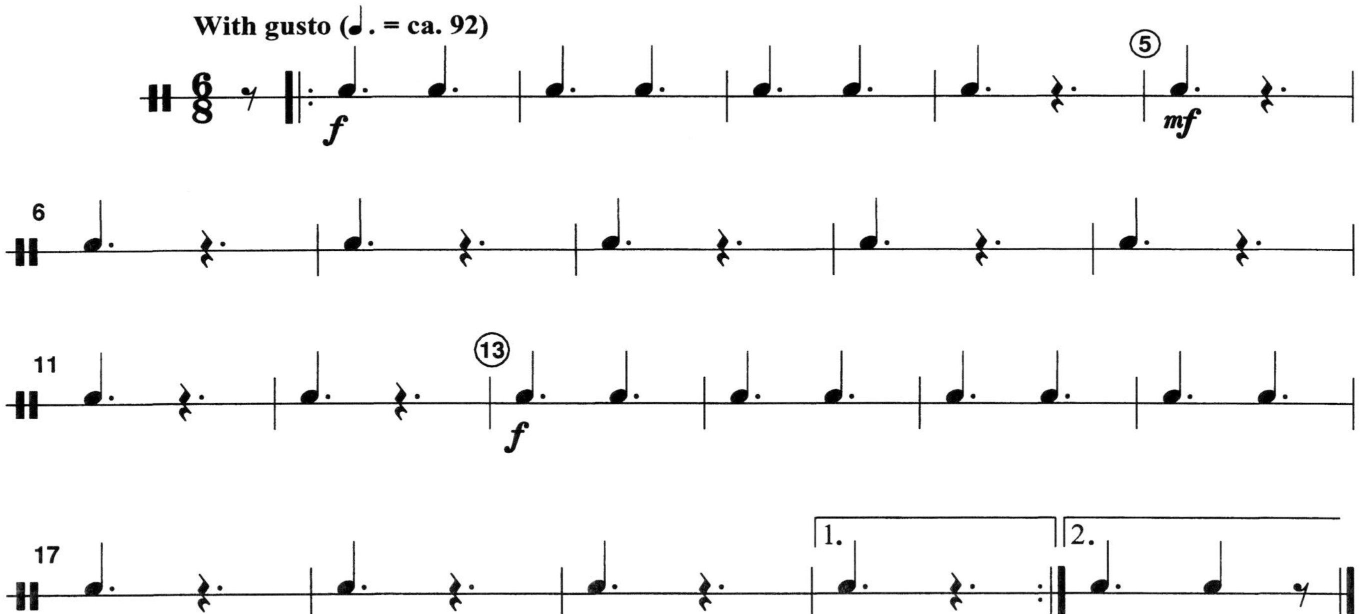

6. I GOT THE BLUES

6. I GOT THE BLUES

CYMBALS

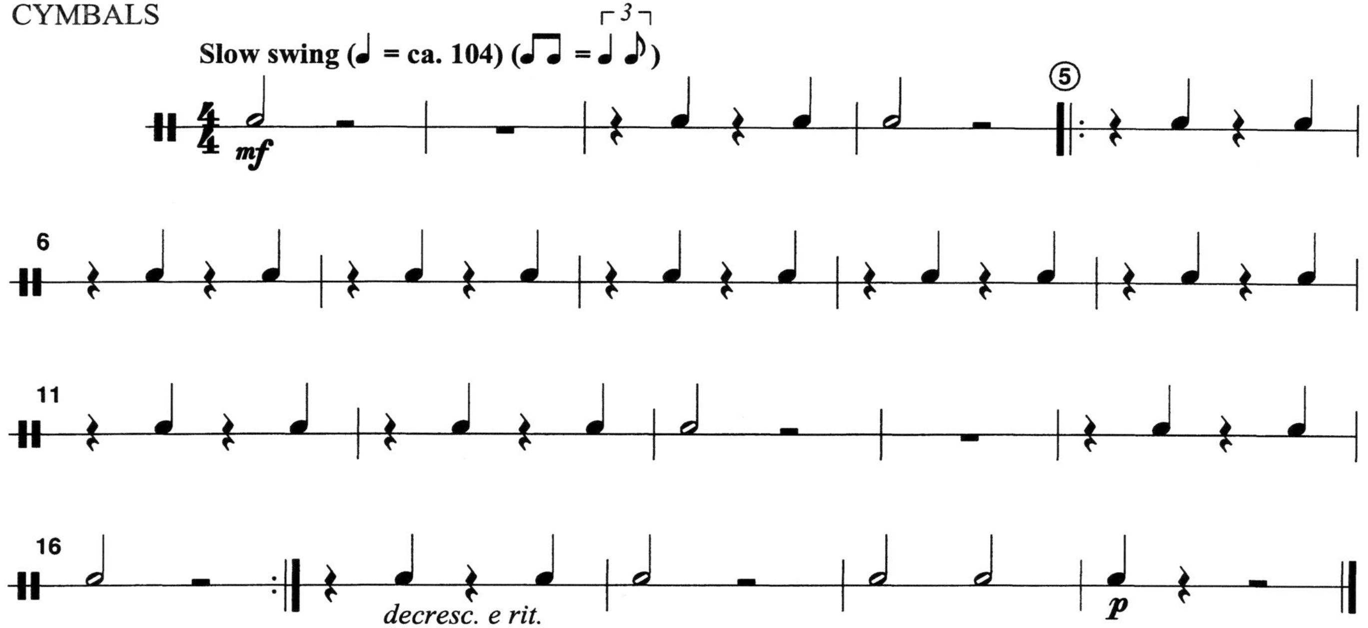

DRUMS

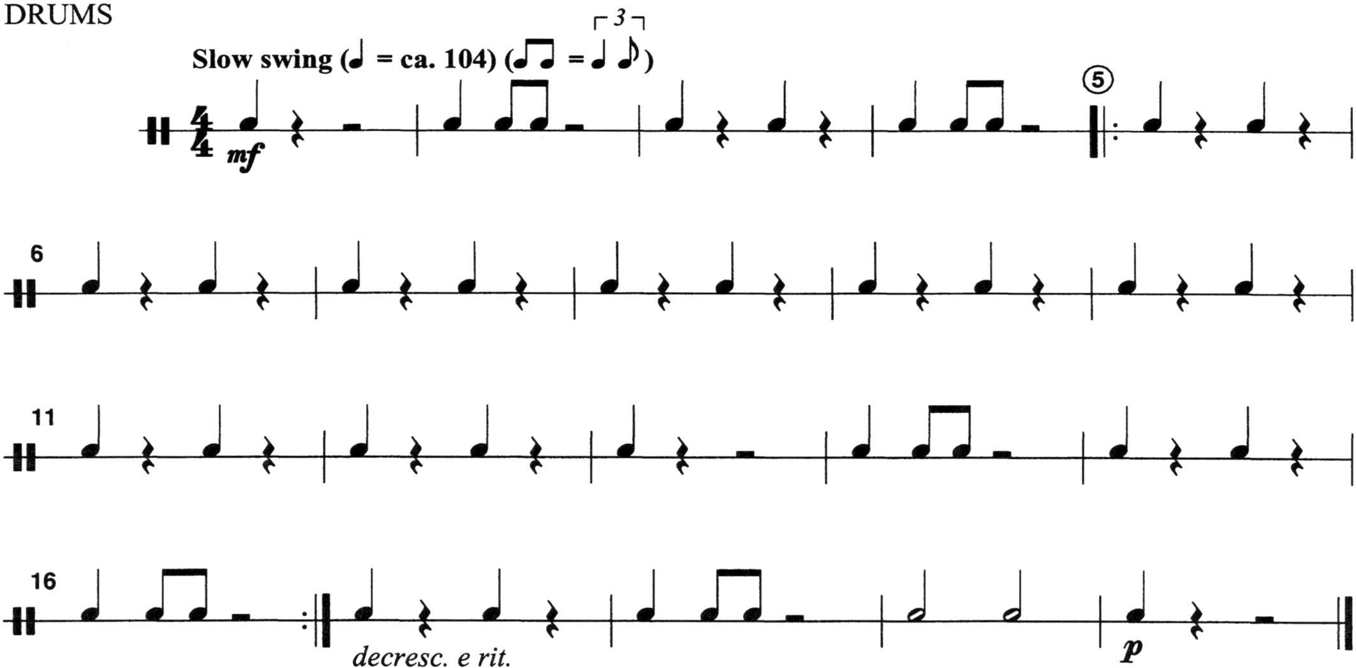

7. WE WANT TO HEAR A WALTZ

BELLS and TRIANGLE

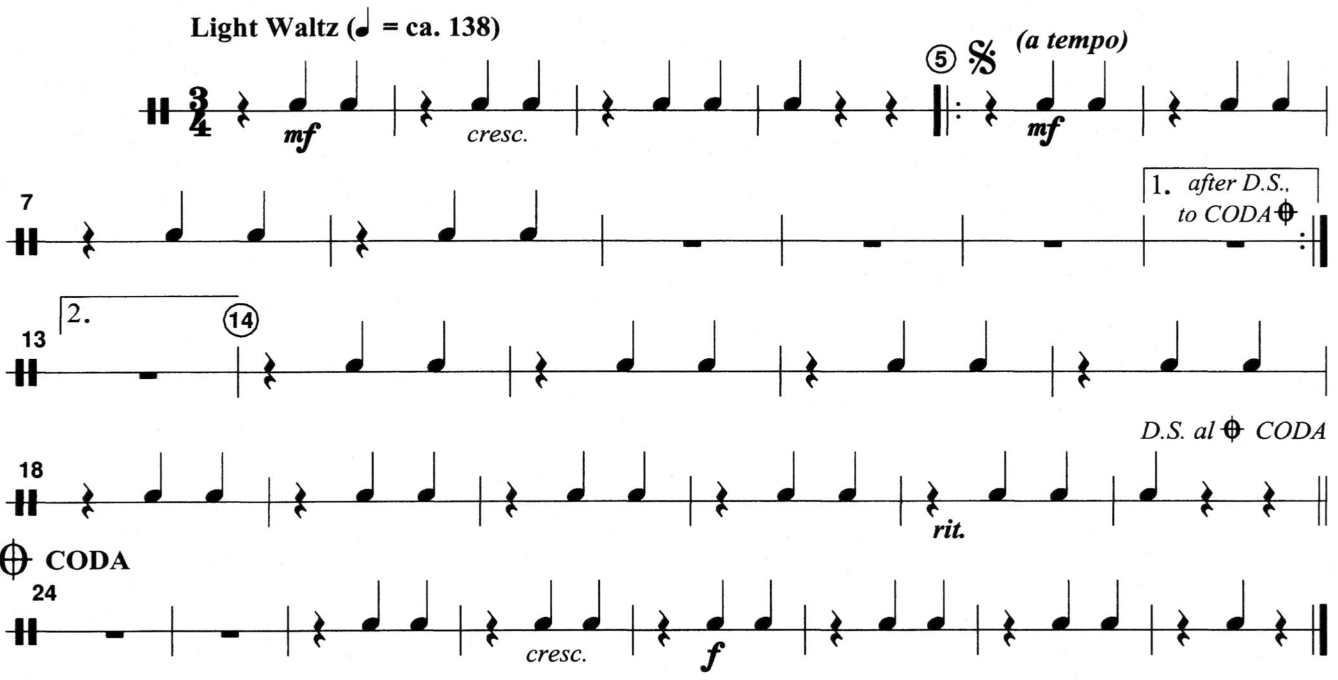

STICKS, WOOD BLOCKS, and CLAVES

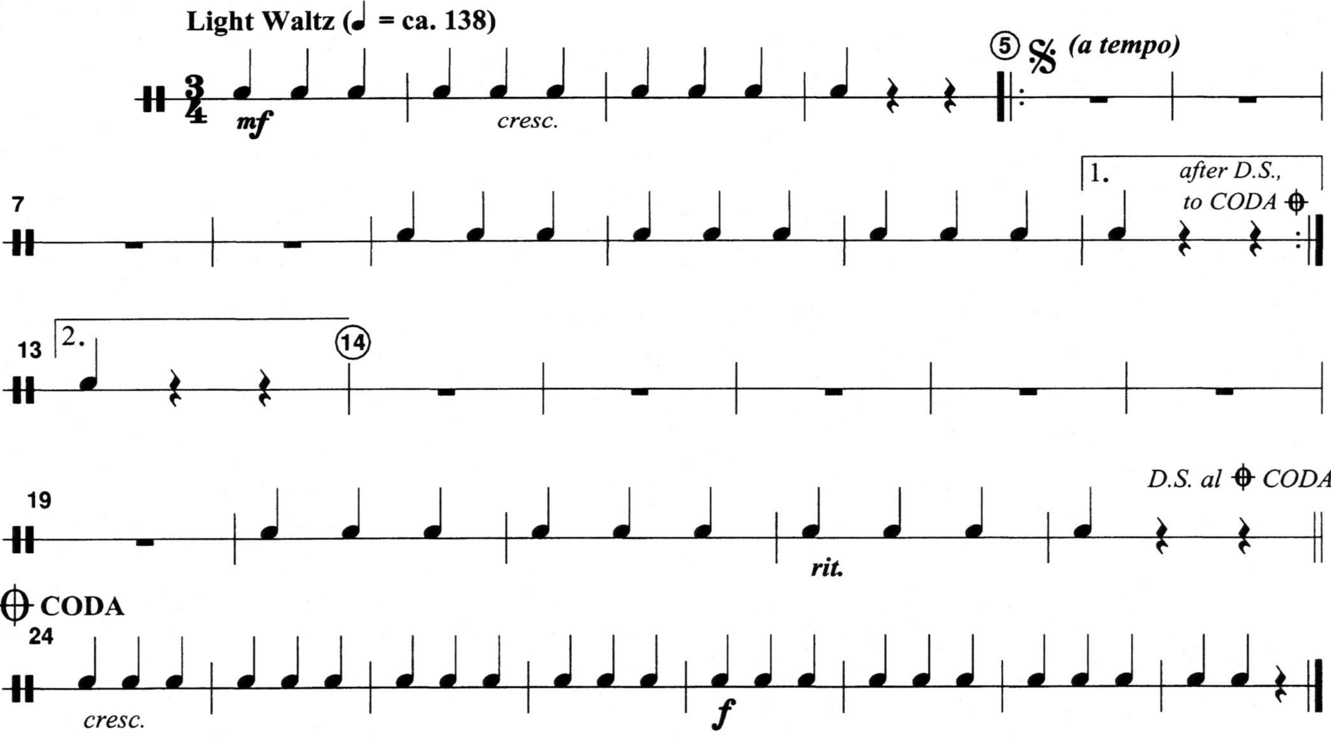

7. WE WANT TO HEAR A WALTZ

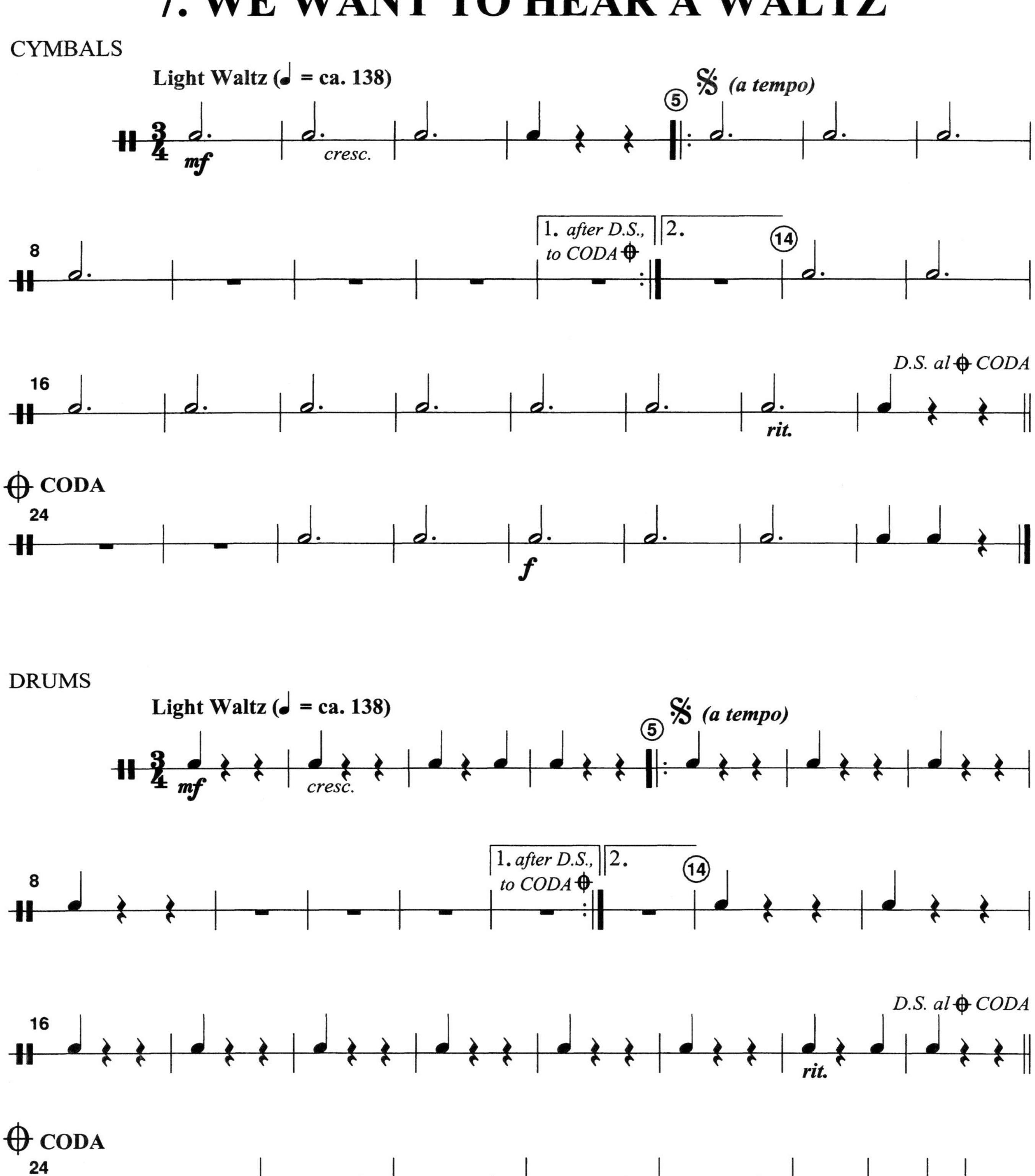

8. CALYPSO!

MARACAS
Latin-feel (♩ = ca. 120-126)
STICKS, WOOD BLOCK, and CLAVES
Latin-feel (♩ = ca. 120-126)

8. CALYPSO!

BELLS, TRIANGLE, and TAMBOURINE

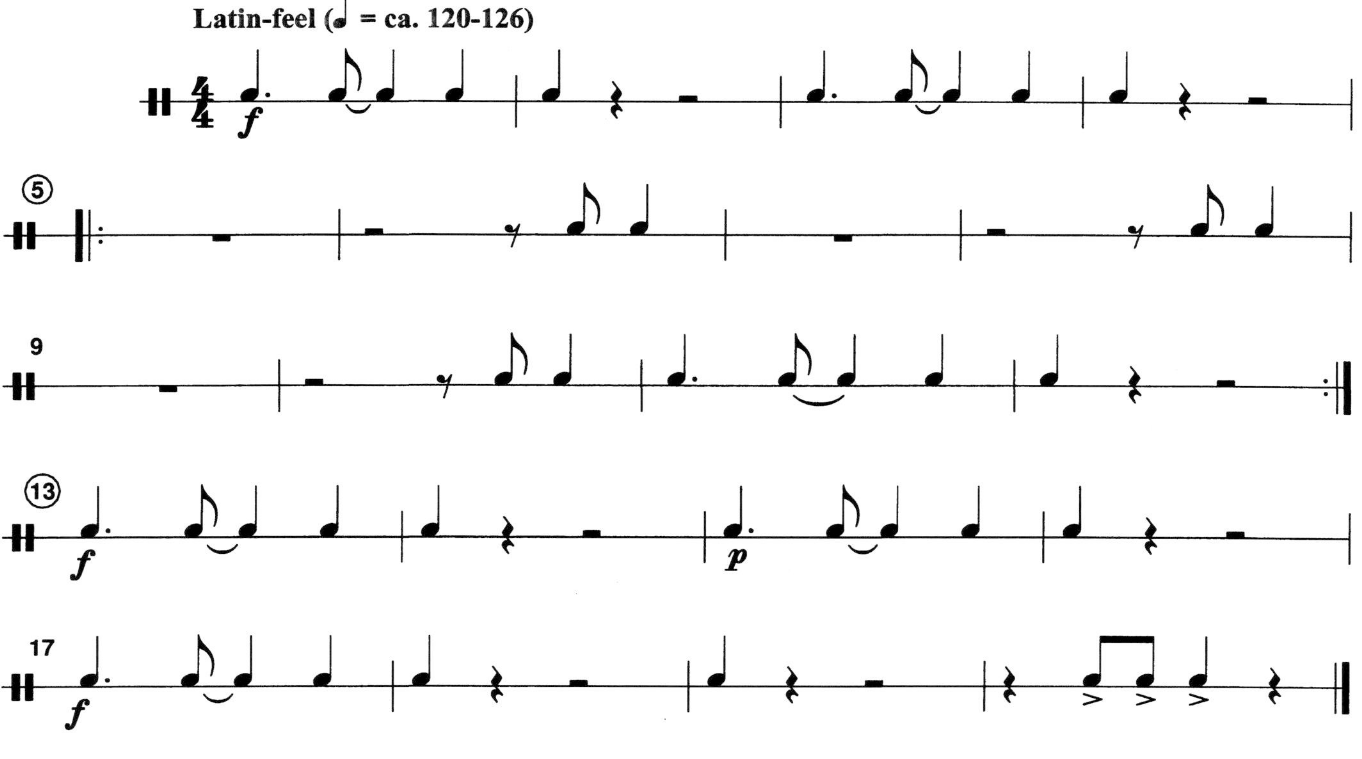

DRUMS and CYMBALS

9. SLOW ROCK AND ROLL

9. SLOW ROCK AND ROLL

CYMBALS and TAMBOURINE

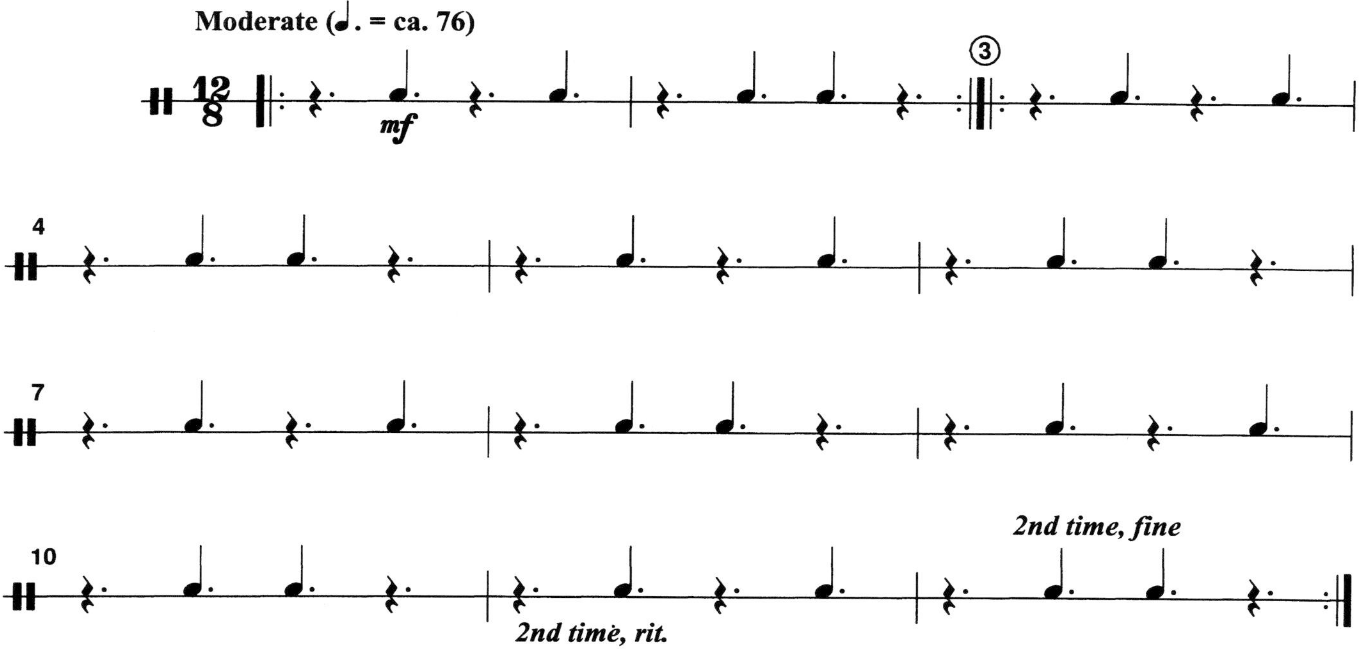

DRUMS

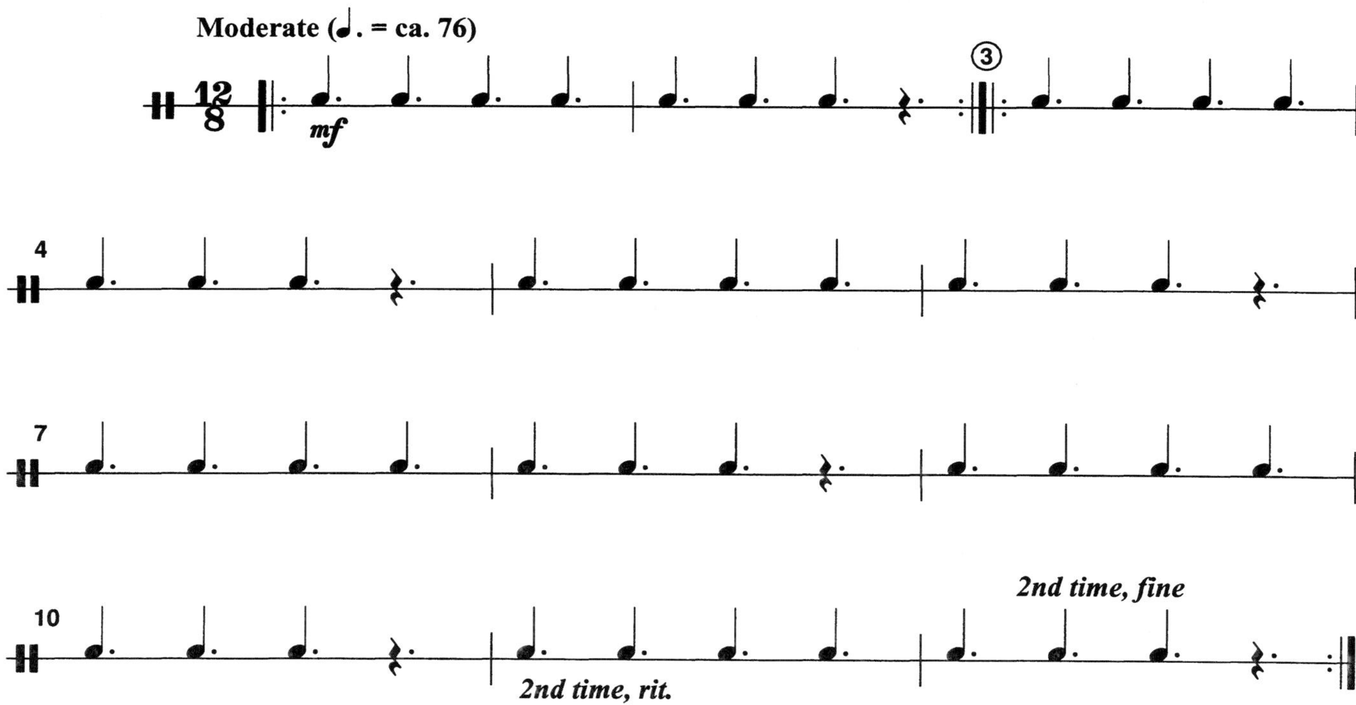

10. OUR COUNTRY HOEDOWN

10. OUR COUNTRY HOEDOWN

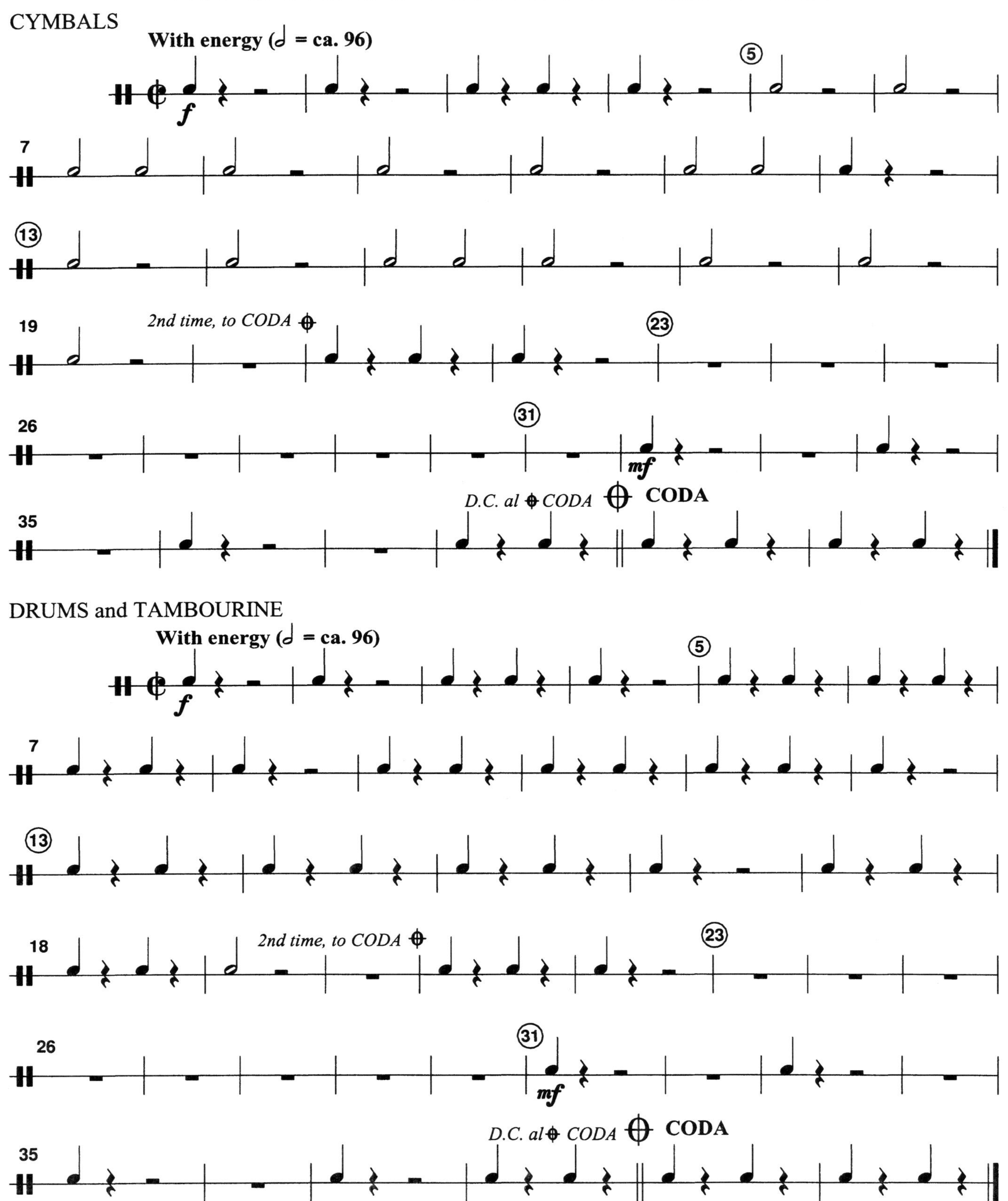

Sally K. Albrecht

SALLY K. ALBRECHT is presently the Director of School Choral Publications for ALFRED PUBLISHING CO., INC. She is a popular choral conductor, composer and clinician, especially known for her work with choral movement. Sally is the author of two books on the subject–*Choral Music in Motion, Volumes I* and *II*, distributed by Alfred.

An annual recipient of the ASCAP Special Music Award since 1987, Sally has over 100 popular choral publications in print (including *The Reindeer Rap, For the Children* and *No Need to Knock!*), four children's musicals (*A Small Part of the World, SuperClaus!, The Night the Reindeer Rocked* and *Santa's Shopping Network*), and two children's songbooks (*Everyday Songs* and *Rhythm to the Rescue!*). Her composition *We Are the Children* was selected to open the 1994 MENC "World's Largest Concert," involving more than eight million singers. She also directed and staged the half-time show singers performing during the 1995 and 1996 Florida Citrus Bowls.

A native of Cleveland, Ohio, Sally received a B.A. degree from Rollins College with a double major in Music and Theatre. From there she moved to the University of Miami where she received both an M.A. in Drama and an M.M. in Accompanying. Her previous employment includes serving as the school choral editor at Shawnee Press, and teaching in the Music Departments at Oakland University and Jersey City State College. She has worked with literally thousands of teachers and students through clinics, conventions and workshops in 40 states, Canada, Singapore and Australia.

Sally and her husband, composer/arranger Jay Althouse, currently reside on Hilton Head Island, SC.

About the Recording

Rhythm to the Rescue!
was recorded at

Noteworthy Studios
Manhattan Beach, Ca

Alan Billingsley - Instrumental Arranger and Producer

Singers

Alison Beatty	Austin Chase	Julia Grove	Christine Schillinger
Alex Smith	John Stehey	Elia Tytell	Samantha Tytell